GLIMPSES OF INDIAN BIRDS

GLIMPSES OF INDIAN BIRDS

DOUGLAS DEWAR

GYAN

Published by

Gyan Publishing House
5, Ansari Road
Daryaganj, New Delhi-110002
Phone: 011-47034999, 9811692060
E-mail: books@gyanbooks.com

Distribution Network
gyanbooks.com
India, USA, Canada, UK, Australia

ISBN: 978-93-7447-079-4 (PB)

First Published, 1913

2nd Impression 2025

Printed at: Gyan Press, Delhi.

GLIMPSES OF INDIAN BIRDS
Author: DOUGLAS DEWAR

GLIMPSES OF INDIAN BIRDS

GLIMPSES OF INDIAN BIRDS

BY DOUGLAS DEWAR

LONDON: JOHN LANE THE BODLEY HEAD
NEW YORK: JOHN LANE COMPANY
TORONTO: BELL & COCKBURN MCMXIII

I DEDICATE

THIS BOOK TO

THEODORE ROOSEVELT

A HUNTER OF BIG GAME AND A NATURALIST

WHO, HAVING BROUGHT COMMON-SENSE TO BEAR

ON THE PROBLEMS OF NATURAL HISTORY

DECLINES TO BE DICTATED TO BY THOSE WHO

HAVE CONSTITUTED THEMSELVES

ZOOLOGICAL AUTHORITIES

PREFACE

IN the brief sketches that follow I find occasion repeatedly to attack the prevalent theories of protective colouration, because it is impossible for the naturalist who uses his eyes to accept these theories.

Most of these hypotheses were advanced by field naturalists, but they have since been elaborated by cabinet zoologists and have become a creed. Now, Huxley remarked with truth, "Science commits suicide when it adopts a creed." With equal truth he asserted, "'Authorities,' 'disciples,' and 'schools' are the curse of science and do more to interfere with the work of the scientific spirit than all its enemies."

In England zoology is at present in the hands of 'schools' and 'authorities' of the kind to which Huxley objected.

The result is that where, in some of my previous books, I have exposed the shallowness of the prevalent theories, I have been taken to task by certain reviewers who are disciples of those 'authorities.' These gentlemen term my criticisms superficial, but they have made no attempt to show in what way my criticisms are superficial. There is a good reason for this. It is that these journalists know well that any attempts to rebut my statements will lead to a controversy in which they cannot but be worsted because the facts are against them.

If what I say is incorrect my reviewers now have an excellent opportunity to demonstrate this.

Lest these have recourse to the unfailing resort of the defeated Darwinian or Wallaceian—the argument of ignorance, lest they say that it is only owing to their insufficient knowledge of Indian birds that they cannot answer me, let me assert that what I say of Indian birds is equally true of British birds.

I assert with confidence that the colouring of nine out of ten birds has some feature which the theories attacked by me cannot account for.

"Hypotheses," wrote Huxley, "are not ends but means. . . . The most useful of servants to the man of science, they are the worst of masters, and when the establishment of the hypotheses comes the end, and fact is attended to only so far as it suits the 'Idee,' science has no longer anything to do with the business."

The hypotheses which I decline to accept have become the masters of many zoologists who are busily occupied in distorting facts which do not coincide with theory.

It is not very long since an English scientific paper published an article entitled "What have ornithologists done for Darwinism?" So long as zoologists test the work of the naturalist by the amount of evidence he collects for Darwinism or any other "ism," it is hopeless to expect zoological science to progress.

CONTENTS

THESE "Glimpses" originally appeared in one or other of the following periodicals: *The Madras Mail, Pioneer, Civil and Military Gazette, Times of India, Bird Notes.*

The author takes this opportunity of thanking the editors of the above papers for permission to reproduce the sketches.

GLIMPSES OF INDIAN BIRDS

GLIMPSES OF INDIAN BIRDS

I

BIRDS IN A GROVE

THE small groves that usually surround hamlets in Oudh are favourite resorts of birds.

I know of few more pleasant ways of passing an hour than under the trees in such a grove at the beginning of December, when the weather is perfect. The number of birds that show themselves is truly astonishing.

Recently I tarried for a little time in such a grove consisting of half a dozen mango trees, a tamarind and a pipal, and witnessed there a veritable avian pageant—a pageant accompanied by music.

The sunbirds (*Arachnechthra asiatica*) were the leading minstrels. There may have been a dozen of them in the little tope. To count them was impossible, because sunbirds are never still for two seconds together. When not flitting about amid the foliage looking for insects they are playing hide-and-seek, or pouring out their canary-like song. At this season of the year the cocks are in undress plumage. In his full splendour the male is glistening purple; but in August he loses nearly all his purple gloss and becomes brownish above and ashy grey below, save for a purple stripe running downwards from his chin. The hen is at all times brown above and yellow below.

The red-whiskered bulbuls (*Otocompsa emeria*) were as numerous and as full of life and motion as the sun-birds. Their tinkling notes mingled pleasantly with the sharper tones of the other choristers.

It is superfluous to state that two or three pairs of doves were in that little *bagh*, and that one or other of them never ceased to coo.

Further, it goes without saying that there were red-starts in that tope. The Indian redstart (*Ruticilla rufiventris*) is one of the commonest birds in Oudh during the winter months. During flight it looks like a little ball of fire, because of its red tail: hence its old English name, fire-tail.

At intervals, a curious *tew* emanated from the foliage. A short search sufficed to reveal the author—the black-headed oriole (*Oriolus melanocephalus*), a glorious golden bird having the head and neck black and some black in the wing. This creature seems never to descend to the ground; it dwells always in the greenwood tree and its life is one long search for fruit, caterpillars and other creeping things.

The flycatchers were a pageant in themselves; there were more species in that tiny *bagh* than are to be found in the whole of Great Britain and Ireland.

First and foremost the fan-tailed flycatcher (*Rhipi-*

dura albifrontata)—the prima donna of the tope—presented herself. Like a fairy in a pastoral play, she comes into view from some leafy bower, announcing her appearance by five or six joyous notes that mount and descend the musical scale. Dainty as a wagtail she is arrayed in black and white like some motacillas. She is dancer as well as singer, and she pirouettes up and down a horizontal branch, bowing now to right and now to left, spreading her tail into a fan and suddenly breaking off her dance to make a flight after an insect.

Even more beautiful was the next flycatcher to introduce itself—Tickell's blue flycatcher (*Cyornis tickelli*). The upper parts of this exquisite little creature are glistening royal blue; the throat and breast are flaming orange, and the lower parts are white. After flitting from bough to bough in search of quarry, it stood still and uttered its lay, which consists of a *chik, chik,* followed by a little trill, not unlike that of the fan-tailed flycatcher. Having delivered itself of its melody, it vanished into the green canopy. Its place was taken almost immediately by a red-breasted flycatcher (*Siphia parva*), a bird very like the English robin in appearance. Ere long it moved away.

Shortly after another flycatcher took its little part in the pageant. This was the grey-headed flycatcher (*Culicicapa ceylonensis*), "a tiny brownie bird," with the head grey and the lower parts bright yellow. With the exception of the *Rhipidura*, all these flycatchers had come down from the Himalayas.

While watching their graceful movements, my

attention was attracted by a curious grating sound that emanated from the branches immediately over my head. On looking up, I saw a crow-pheasant (*Centropus rufipennis*) running up a branch in the inimitable manner of his kind. His bright red eye was fixed on me, and he had evidently made up his cuculine mind that " distance lends enchantment to the view " of a human being, and accordingly lost no time in making his exit.

Scarcely had I lost sight of him when there was a considerable commotion in the pipal tree near by. When running to discover the cause of this I startled half a dozen pipits (*Anthus rufulus*) that, hidden by the grass, were feeding on the ground. They, as is their wont when frightened, flew into the foliage. Pipits are dull brown birds, streaked like larks, that display tail-wagging propensities. I discovered that the bird making the commotion near the summit of the pipal tree was a vulture. Very large and out of place did it seem struggling among the slender branches with wings spread-eagled. It was tugging away vigorously at a small branch and soon succeeded in breaking it off. Having accomplished this, it scrambled on to what looked like a large ball of dried leaves and twigs caught in one of the upper branches. This was a nest in course of construction, which the vulture was lining with pipal branches. Presently the huge bird flew off, and I was then able to identify it as the white-backed vulture (*Pseudogyps bengalensis*). I returned to the mango tree beneath which I had been standing, and in so doing disturbed a bee-eater (*Merops viridis*) that was perching on one of the lower branches. Of the presence in the vicinity of these charming little birds I was already aware from their soft twitterings. I had not actually seen them, because their habit is to perch on the outer branches of trees, whence they make aerial sallies after insects.

The calls of the blossom-headed parakeets (*Palæornis cyanocephalus*), far softer and mellower than those of the rose-ringed species, had at frequent intervals mingled with the notes of the other birds; and at this moment one of these green parrots settled on a branch quite close to me. Her slate-coloured head showed her to be a hen; in this species the head of the cock is coloured like a ripe plum.

Sharp sounds, like those made by insects, issuing from every tree revealed the presence of warblers. These birds were so small and so active that I am not certain to what species they belonged. The majority of them were, I believe, willow warblers (*Phylloscopus tristis*).

At intervals the *to-wee to-wee* of the tailor-bird (*Orthotomus sutorius*) had rung out clear and distinct from the medley of sounds that filled the grove. Suddenly two tailor-birds came on the scene, one chasing the other. They alighted on a horizontal bough, where they tarried sufficiently long to enable me to see the chestnut crown so characteristic of the species.

I have omitted to make mention of the sprightly magpie-robin (*Copsychus saularis*). Of this species there was at least one pair in that little grove, and several times did the cock descend to the ground, and hop about, with tail erect. He is arrayed in black and white, and a smarter-looking bird does not exist. His mate also put in an appearance; she has all his sprightliness and is equally tastefully attired in grey and white.

Having spent an hour in the grove, I had to return to my tent to work, without having witnessed all the *dramatis personæ* of the daily pageant. As I was leaving the tope a hen brown-backed robin (*Thamnobia cambaiensis*) hopped out of an *arhar* field and stood beneath a mango tree, carrying her tail erect so as to display the red undertail coverts.

After I had reached my tent, fifty yards away, I heard the *kutur—kutur—kuturuk* of the green barbet (*Thereiceryx zeylonicus*), the loud tap, tap, tap of the golden-backed woodpecker (*Brachypternus aurantius*), and the cheerful notes of the king crow (*Dicrurus ater*).

II

THE MAGPIE-ROBIN

THE magpie-robin (*Copsychus saularis*), or *dhayal*, as the Indians call him, is a truly delightful bird. He is of handsome appearance, bold disposition, and confiding habits. He is, further, a singer who can hold his own in any company when at his best. The *dhayal* is a typically Indian bird, being found in all parts of the country from the Himalayas to Cape Comorin. He is common in Ceylon and ascends the hills of India to altitudes of over 6000 feet. He is, I believe, more abundant in the United Provinces than anywhere else. It is no exaggeration to assert that at least one pair of magpie-robins lives in every garden in Oudh and Agra. I do not count as gardens those treeless compounds in which some bungalows are situate, for the magpie-robin is a bird that loves shade. The species, although by no means rare in South India, is not nearly so abundant there as in the northern part of the peninsula.

The *dhayal* is very easily identified. The cock is a black and white bird rather larger than the familiar English robin. His head, neck, breast, and upper parts are black with a white bar in the wing. The lower parts are white, as are the outer tail feathers.

The above description will show that the black and white markings of the plumage are similar to those of the common magpie; hence the popular name of the bird—magpie-robin. If the distribution of the magpie-robin happened to coincide with that of the magpie, I have no doubt whatever that zoologists of the school of Wallace would cite the *dhayal* as an example of protective mimicry. They would tell us that this robin had aped the dress of the powerful magpie in order to dupe the crows and other bullying birds that vex the lives of their smaller neighbours.

As the magpie-robin dwells mostly where the magpie is not found, no Wallaceian has attempted to explain why its colouring is so like that of the magpie. As a matter of fact, the magpie scheme of colouring seems to be a popular one in nature (if I may be permitted to use such an expression). It appears in seven species which are in no way closely related one to another, to wit, a goose, a crow, a tanager, a honey-eater, a swallow-shrike, a robin, and, of course, the common magpie.

The hen magpie-robin is brownish grey where her lord and master is black, the pattern of her plumage being the same as his.

The magpie-robin does not carry his tail as most birds do, but goes about with it pointed to the sky. This gives the bird a very sprightly appearance. Its actions fulfil the promise of its looks. It is never still for an instant. Now it descends to the ground, where it hops about with tail erect, picking up here and there tiny insects; now it flies into a tree or bush, where it pursues its search for insects or pours forth its joyous song. Nor does it confine its operations to trees, bushes, and dry land. I have seen a magpie-robin hunting for insects on a tangled mass of weeds and stems floating on water. On these it hopped about just as it does on *terra firma*. Each little jump caused considerable commotion in the water. The bird did not seem to mind its toes getting wet.

The *dhayal* is essentially a bird of gardens. Like the English robin, it prefers to dwell as near human habitations as possible. In my opinion it is one of the finest song birds in the world. Like the majority of melodious birds, the magpie-robin is not in song all the year round. During the early winter it is a silent creature. Towards the end of the cold weather the cock begins to find his voice, and at that time his efforts are not very pleasing to the human ear. But each successive day's effort produces better results, until, by March, the bird is able to pour forth a torrent of far-reaching melody which is inferior to that of no Indian bird save his cousin, the shama.

Needless to say, the period when the cock *dhayal* is in song corresponds to the mating time. At this season the cocks are very pugnacious. This pugnacity is simply the expression of the fact that the *dhayal* is at that time more than usually overflowing with energy. This energy has to find outlets. One of these is through the medium of vigorous song. Another way of dissipating energy is by performing gymnastic feats in the air. As a rule magpie-robins rarely perform sustained flights. They are content with flitting from bush to bush, or making little excursions to the ground and back again. But at the breeding season the cocks often fly up high in the air and describe a series of wide circles. They will spend hours in this performance with only a few seconds' rest at long intervals.

The eggs are nearly always placed in some natural hole, that is to say, one not excavated by the *dhayal* itself. The hole is sometimes in a tree, but nine times out of ten in Northern India the site selected is a hole in some building. The servants' quarters in the corner of some shady garden are almost invariably chosen. A very favourite spot is between the wooden lintel and the mud wall of a *kachcha* building ; such buildings are well called *kachcha*, for they begin to crack and fall down as soon as they are built. The cracks and crevices that appear in them offer just what magpie-robins want for nesting purposes. The eggs are not laid on the bare brick, mud, or other material in which the cavity exists. The hole is invariably lined with roots, fibres, grass, feathers, or any other soft material available. My experience of the nests of this species has been confined chiefly to Northern India, and I do not recollect ever having found a nest that was not in the wall of some building ; but observers from South India say that, as often as not, the *dhayal* nests in trees.[1] Oates states that in Burma the magpie-robin almost invariably selects a large hollow bamboo, and

[1] Such is the contrariness of birds in general and of magpie-robins in particular, that since this book went to press I have found in the Pilibhit and Bareilly districts no fewer than seven *dhayals'* nests in holes in trees!

places its nest about two feet inside, near the first joint; but he adds that the bamboos selected are generally to be found lying about the verandahs and cucumber framings of the native houses. The truth of the matter would seem to be that magpie-robins select the very first cavity of the right size they come across, and, as they affect human habitations, the cavity used is almost invariably near some man's dwelling. In Northern India the construction of the dwellings of Indians is such that the walls afford convenient sites, so that these are generally utilised; in other parts of the country, where the walls do not present so many holes, other cavities in trees, etc., are selected.

The eggs have a greenish-white background which is usually largely obliterated by blotches of brownish red. March, April, May, and June are the months in which eggs are most likely to be found; April and May for preference.

III

THE INDIAN SNAKE-BIRD

THE Indian darter, or snake-bird (*Plotus melanogaster*) is best described by what I may perhaps call the synthetic method. Take a large cormorant and remove the head and neck; to the headless cormorant, sew on the head and neck of a heron, and you will have produced a very fair imitation of the Indian snake-bird. If during the operation you happen to have dislocated one of the lower neck vertebrae of the heron, so much the better, for the slender neck of the darter is characterised by a bend at the junction of the eighth and ninth vertebrae, which, as Mr. Garrod has shown, enables the bird, by suddenly straightening the neck, to transfix the fish on which it has designs. As a catcher of fish the snake-bird is probably without peer. This is not surprising, since it possesses the swimming and diving apparatus of the cormorant, the long neck and dagger-like beak of the heron, and, in addition, a patent thrusting apparatus in the shape of the aforesaid kink in the neck.

The Indian darter is a bird with which all who go down to *jhils* to shoot duck must be familiar, since it is a full yard in length and occurs in most parts of India,

Burma, and Ceylon. Notwithstanding its large size, it is apt to be overlooked when in the water, because it almost invariably swims with the body submerged, showing only the upper neck above the surface. Every now and again it completely disappears from view. After remaining submerged for several seconds the head reappears with a small fish projecting from the bill. The fish is forthwith thrown a little way into the air, and then caught and swallowed. This habit of tossing food into the air preparatory to swallowing it occurs in many long-billed species, and appears to be the most expeditious method of getting food from the tip of an elongated beak to the other extremity, where it is seized by the muscular walls of the gullet and passed onwards.

The snake-bird is said sometimes to secure its quarry by diving from a perch like a kingfisher. I have not observed the bird behave thus, and the method does not appear to be generally practised.

Plotus melanogaster is called the snake-bird because of its long, slender, snake-like neck, which looks very like the anterior portion of a water-snake when the bird swims, as it often does, with the body submerged. If danger threatens the bird usually sinks in the water until every part of it except the beak disappears. This certainly is a method of hiding superior to that said to be adopted by the ostrich.

The snake-bird is a rapid swimmer, and as it frequently remains under water for thirteen or fourteen seconds at a time, it is able to move considerable distances while completely submerged.

The snake-bird is a powerful flier. While on the wing it does not retract its neck after the manner of the heron, but progresses with neck extended. The neck being so slender gives the bird a comic appearance and renders it easy to identify during flight. When resting from its piscatorial labours it betakes itself to the edge of the *jhil* or to an islet and squats there to dry its plumage in the approved cormorant fashion, with wings partially, and tail fully, expanded. In this grotesque attitude it frequently preens itself, and, thanks to the length of its neck and bill, it has not to undergo the contortions that characterise most birds when trying to reach with the tip of the beak their least accessible feathers.

The Indian darter does not appear to patronise the open sea. Probably it objects to the swell and finds its quarry easier to catch in comparatively shallow water. It does not mind salt water, for it may be found in tidal estuaries and creeks. I have seen it on the Cooum at Madras. It is, however, essentially a bird of the *jhil*. Needless to state that it is no songster—none of the *Phalacocoracidae* are melodious—nor is it given to undue loquacity, but it is capable, when the occasion demands, of emitting a harsh croak.

So far as my experience goes, snake-birds usually occur singly or in pairs, but according to Jerdon hundreds of the birds are to be seen on some *jhils* in Bengal.

At the nesting season it is more likely to be seen in flocks than at other times, for numbers breed together, often in company with herons and cormorants. Like these latter, the snake-bird times its nesting operations so that the young will be hatched out after the monsoon has brought into existence numbers of amphibia and crustacea on which to feed them. Accordingly, it nidificates in July, August, and September in Northern India and Travancore, which are served by the south-west monsoon, and in January and February in those parts of South India visited by the north-east monsoon.

The nest is a mere platform of twigs, usually placed in low trees, babools for preference, and growing in situations flooded in the rains.

I do not know of any place near the city of Madras where snake-birds breed. Mr. T. F. Bourdillon, writing of Travancore, says, "I once found a colony of these birds nesting above the Athirapuzha in the Kodasheri River in September. They had taken possession of an island in midstream, where they had built their untidy nests on small trees about twenty feet high, and there were fresh and hard-set eggs in them in all stages of incubation, while half-fledged birds scrambled about the branches or flopped into the water at our approach. The nests were about one foot in diameter and roughly built of twigs. The eggs are white and covered with a chalky coat and measure 2 inches by 1¼. Some of the eggs are rather larger at one end than the other, while others are truly fusiform with pointed ends."

The snake-bird is sometimes kept as a pet by Indians. According to Mr. J. R. Cripps the Buddeas, a race of gipsies who travel about the Eastern Bengal districts in boats, are very fond of keeping these birds, almost every boat tenanted by these gipsies having a snake-bird on board.

The shoulder feathers of the Indian darter are long and narrow like the hackles of a cock. Each is black with a conspicuous silvery shaft, which renders it a thing of unusual beauty. According to Jerdon these feathers constitute the badge of royalty among the Khasias, and used to be the badge of one of the Bengal Regiments of Irregular Cavalry.

IV

MINIVETS

WERE a beauty show held open to all the birds of India, the minivets would, I think, win the first prize. To say this is to bestow high praise, for India teems with beautiful birds.

All the colours of the rainbow appear in our avian population. Indeed, the Indian pitta (*Pitta brachyura*) —the bird of nine colours—is a rainbow in himself, displaying as he does red, yellow, grey, and various shades of blue and green, to say nothing of black and white.

Most of our beautiful birds, however, pin their affections more especially to one colour. The parakeets, the chloropses, the green pigeons, the bee-eaters, and the barbets wear sufficient green to satisfy the most patriotic Irishman.

Golden yellow is affected by the orioles and the ioras.

The kingfisher, the roller and the purple porphyrio are as blue as Putney on boat-race day.

Sunbirds, pheasants, and peafowl favour us with a gorgeous display of metallic hues.

The rose-coloured starling and the flamingo wear their pink as proudly as a Westminster boy.

The minivets are the leaders of fashion as regards the reds and yellows. The cocks vie with the hens as to who shall be the more resplendent, and, in so doing, make short work of the attempts of Wallace and Darwin to explain sexual difference in plumage. In most species of minivets the cocks are arrayed in bright scarlet, whence the name Cardinal-bird, rich crimson, deep rose colour, flaming red, or soft orange, while their respective wives are studies in the various shades of yellow. But the beauty of the minivet is not merely that of colouring. The elegance of its slender, well-proportioned form rivals that of the wagtail.

Minivets are little birds with longish tails which flit about among the leaves of trees in flocks of half a dozen, conversing in low but exceedingly melodious tones.

They are veritable nomads. They never remain long in one place, except, of course, when nesting. Without apparently ever taking a prolonged flight, the flocks of minivets must traverse very considerable tracts of country. They never leave the neighbourhood of trees. Their habit is to pass methodically from tree to tree, tarrying awhile at each, seeking for insects now on the topmost branches, where the dainty forms of the birds stand out sharp and clear against the azure sky, now lost to view amid the denser foliage.

Few are the lurking insects that escape the bright little eye of the minivet. Even those resting on parts of the tree where a bird cannot obtain a foothold do not escape, for the minivet is able to seize them while hovering in the air on vibrating wings. Occasionally, in order to reach a tiny victim hidden away on the under surface of a leaf, the minivet will hang by its feet, like a titmouse, from the slender branch that bears the leaf. At times the minivet will indulge in a little zigzag flight among the green branches, and it is on such occasions that the cock utters his feeble but pleasing little warble.

Fifteen species of minivet adorn India. Unfortunately, most of them are of comparatively restricted range, being confined to the Himalayas. Two species only, I believe, are common in South India, namely, the small minivet (*Pericrocotus peregrinus*) and the orange minivet (*P. flammeus*). The former is the only one likely to be seen in Madras city. If we would see the orange species we must go to the Nilgiris or the Western Ghauts.

Both sexes of *Pericrocotus peregrinus* are handsome without being showy. They are about the size of sparrows, but have a much longer tail. The head, nape, and upper part of the back of the cock are of a rich slaty-grey tint, which deepens into black on the sides of the head, and on the throat, wings, and tail. There is an orange bar in the wing, and the tail feathers are tipped with that colour. The breast and lower portion of the back are of the richest scarlet. The female is less showily attired than the cock ; she lacks his scarlet trimmings and wears yellow in place of his patches of orange.

The orange minivet is a still more beautiful bird. The head and the back of the cock are black. His wings are black and flame-coloured red, the red being so arranged as to form a band running along, not across, the wing during flight. This longitudinal red or yellow wing-band characterises most species of minivet. His tail feathers are all red, save the two median ones, which are black. During flight the brilliant red seems almost to obliterate the black, so that a number of cocks, as they fly from one tree to another, look like sparks driven before the wind. The hen is marked in the same way as the cock, but in her the flaming red colour is replaced by bright yellow. In my opinion, "orange" is not a very suitable adjective to apply to this species. A literal translation of the Latin name—the flame-coloured minivet—would be more appropriate.

A minivet's nest is a work of art. As all the species construct precisely the same kind of nursery, what is true of any one species applies equally to all the others. The nest is a neat little cup, about three inches in diameter, composed of twigs and grasses, and covered outside with moss and cobwebs, so that in colour and general appearance the exterior is exactly like the bark of a tree. It is usually placed on a bough; if this happens to be a thick one, the nest is totally invisible to any person looking up into the tree. If the branch happens to be a thin one, the nursery, seen from below, looks exactly like a knot or swelling in the branch. Thus, unless one actually sees the minivet sitting on the nest, or climbs the tree, it is scarcely possible to locate the little nursery. It is easy enough to discover that a pair have a nest, for the parent birds make a great noise when a human being comes anywhere near. If they happen to be carrying food in the beak for the young birds, they at once drop it, set up their cry of distress and try to entice the stranger away by flying a little distance off. If this ruse[1] be not successful, the hen minivet will act as if her wing were broken and flap along away from the nest.

It is an interesting fact that although minivets build open nests and the sexes differ so considerably in appearance, both the cock and the hen take part in incubation.

Some years ago, when writing of the small minivet, I quoted Mr. William Jesse as describing a very curious phenomenon in connection with the nesting of this species, namely that in his experience almost invariably two hens and one cock take part in nest building and incubation. "What is the exact duty of this second wife," writes Jesse, "I cannot make out. Possibly she may be a drudge. That she exists I have satisfied myself time after time, and so convinced are the Martiniere boys of the fact that they—no mean observers by the way—rarely trouble to look for a nest if only one female is present. Unfortunately, I have never yet found out what happens when there are young. Whether both females take part in incubation and in rearing the young I do not know. I do not think that both lay eggs, as I have never found more than three." From the time when I first read the above passage I have paid particular attention to minivets,

[1] I use the word "ruse" for want of a better term. I do not believe that the bird *intends* to deceive the intruder. I am disposed to think that this feigning of injury is a purely instinctive act. The phenomenon is discussed on p. 207 *infra*.

with the object of trying to account for the alleged phenomenon, and the result of my efforts is that I have never seen more than one cock and one hen at a nest, whether it be under construction or whether it contain eggs or young. Moreover, I have not come across any naturalist other than Mr. Jesse who has seen more than two birds at the nest. I am therefore driven to the conclusion that minivets are monogamous birds and that the observation recorded by Mr. Jesse is faulty, that the presence of the second female was due to the chance visit of an outsider. Possibly, since there seem to be more hen minivets than cocks, there is considerable competition among the hens for cocks, and it may happen that the hen who has set her cap at a cock in vain may stay on in the vicinity for some time after her rejection.

V

THE POWER OF ANIMALS TO EXPRESS THOUGHT

THE thoughts of birds and beasts are probably few and simple. Yet it is unlikely that they are able to communicate all their thoughts to one another, because the language they possess consists of a few monosyllables, by which they can express only elementary feelings such as pain, anger, fear, hunger, and the presence of food.

Some animals possess a much larger vocabulary than others. Dr. Garner, who went to Africa to study the language of his Simian brothers, found that the average monkey was able to emit only about seven cries, but the vocabulary of the highly intelligent chimpanzee comprised twenty-two separate calls.

According to Mr. Edmund Selous, the rook is really in process of evolving a language. He records no fewer than thirty-three distinct sounds he heard rooks utter, and states that this is but a small page out of their vocabulary. Nevertheless, he is compelled to admit that only in few cases was he able to connect a note with any particular state of mind.

The articulate language of animals is a language of monosyllables, a language composed almost entirely of interjections. Such a language, while very expressive as far as it goes, does not go very far. And the question naturally arises, does it go sufficiently far to meet the needs of the various species, or have they some means of communicating with one another other than by sounds ? It is very tempting to believe that they have, that they are able to transmit thought to one another in some way. It is only on the assumption of brain waves that one can explain the soldier-like evolutions which flocks of birds sometimes perform in the air.

I have often wondered how those species of birds, of which both the cock and hen take part in the nest-building operations, select the site. The matter is, of course, simple when only the one sex constructs the nest. But how is the site selected when both sexes build ? It is tempting to believe that they discuss the matter, that the hen says to the cock, " Now, James, my dear, it is necessary for us to build a nest without delay : come, let us select a secluded spot wherein to build " ; and to picture the little birds hunting about together and criticising the sites each selects. Nevertheless, I think it most unlikely that any such discussion takes place. Nest building is largely instinctive. In the case of the first nest it is improbable that the little builders quite know what they are doing, and I do not see how, before the nest is begun, they can have any idea of what it will look like when it is finished.

It is possible that birds agree as to the site without any discussion or without any communication. Let us suppose that a pair of bulbuls have mated. Suddenly one of them is overmastered by the nest-building instinct which has hitherto lain dormant. This particular bird is impelled by some irresistible force to seek out a site and then forthwith to begin to build the nest. The nest-building instinct of its mate, which is dormant, is at once awakened by the sight of its spouse collecting material. When this happens the second bird begins collecting, and is content to work at the structure already commenced by its mate. Assuming the correctness of the suggestion that the nest-building instinct does not, as a rule, become awakened simultaneously in a pair of birds, what will happen in the exceptional cases when the instinct does awaken simultaneously? When this happens, it is my belief that each sex commences to build a separate nest. When one of the pair discovers what its mate is doing, it, of course, gets angry and scolds it. The other returns the compliment. Probably the next step is that each examines the handiwork of the other and thinks very little of it. Possibly at first each refuses to yield to the other, or the one whose nest is the least advanced leaves this in favour of the other, or—a third alternative—the stronger bird may attack the weaker and compel it to desert its nest.

This, of course, is pure conjecture. But it is in accordance with the fact that numbers of nests are commenced which are never completed, and which, indeed, never progress very far. There are at present in my verandah two nests belonging to bulbuls which have been left after about three hours' work was put into them. Several explanations of this phenomenon are possible. Each bird may have commenced a separate nest, and so one was deserted; or the site in question may have been found to have some fatal defect, consequently the nest has been given up; or the birds have been scared away or killed. The last alternative is the least likely, and I am inclined to believe that the first explanation is the true one.

I recently read in *Country Life* an exceedingly interesting account of the nest-building operations of a pair of wagtails. The account is brief and has so important a bearing on the subject we are discussing that I take the liberty to quote at length :—

"From the cover of a riverside cottage," writes Mr. Alfred Taylor of the grey wagtail in England, "I saw two birds repeatedly fly to a rocky ledge both with nest-building material in their beaks. It was soon evident that the male wagtail had selected one nest and the female another place a couple of yards away. The former for some time took no notice of the doings of his mate, and they both continued to gather materials into their selected places. Suddenly he flew to her position and commenced removing her material to the place where he thought the nest ought to be. Trouble seemed to be brewing in the family, especially when she still persisted in carrying dead grass to her site. In the end the cock bird lost his temper, flew to her ledge, and viciously attacked her, knocking off the ledge all evidence of her efforts at building. She flew away, and for a couple of hours remained perched in a tree and sulked, evidently much upset at her chastisement, not taking the slightest notice of overtures of peace from her mate. As the deadlock seemed likely to continue I departed.

"Two days later I was round again, eager to see how the difference had been settled, if at all. To my great surprise, I must confess, the male bird had given way to the female, and the nearly completed nest was on her chosen site. A close examination of the two places showed that the judgment of the male had been at fault. Where he had erred was in not detecting the presence of mice; it was quite impossible for these destructive little animals to reach the spot selected by the hen."

Here, then, is a case of the cock having selected one site and the hen another. Had they gone about choosing a site in company and disagreed upon the place, it is hardly likely that the cock would for some time have taken no notice of what the hen was doing; he would surely have set his foot down at once. The fact that at first he took no notice seems to show that at the outburst of what I may perhaps call the fury of nest-building the cock had eyes for nothing but his work. Again, when the cock did assert his authority, he apparently did not argue with the hen. He simply knocked her and her handiwork off the ledge—a rude but forcible, if inarticulate, method of expressing his feelings.

It may be asked, how was it that the birds agreed to the change of site if they were not able to communicate with one another? Here, again, we must wander into the field of conjecture. It must suffice that it is possible to explain the change of tactics of the cock without assuming any communication between him and his mate. Let us suppose that while she was sulking, and he was working, a mouse appeared on the scene. This would alarm him, and possibly the instinct of flying from enemies, that the appearance of the mouse called into play, would cause him to desert his nest, and perhaps he too began to sulk. Then the hen, once again overcome by the nest-building instinct, recommenced her work, and when the cock followed suit he left his useless site and worked at hers.

Investigation into the extent to which birds and beasts can communicate with one another is as difficult as it is fascinating. It is one of those subjects of which probably but little can be learned by systematic experiment. The casual observer is as likely to throw light upon it as the man who makes a special study of it. A chance incident, such as that observed by Mr. Taylor, throws a flood of light upon the subject. It is not until we have a large number of such observations on record that we shall be able to acquire some definite knowledge of the extent to which birds and beasts can, and do, communicate with one another.

VI

PIED WOODPECKERS

NO fewer than fifty-six species of woodpecker occur in India, and of these thirteen wear a pied livery. The black-and-white woodpeckers are all small birds. Most of them are of very limited distribution, several being confined to the Himalayas and the connected hills. One species is peculiar to the Andamans. One pied woodpecker, however, ranges from Cochin China, through India, to Ceylon, but its distribution, although wide, is capricious. It is abundant in all parts of North-West India, but is said not to occur in Eastern Bengal and Assam. I do not remember having seen it in Madras, yet it is the common woodpecker of Bombay. The bird is easily identified. A pied woodpecker seen in South India can belong to no species other than that which is known as *Liopicus mahrattensis* to men of science. The English name of this species is the yellow-fronted pied woodpecker. It is clothed in black-and-white raiment set off by a yellow forehead, and, in the case of the cock, a short red crest. There is also a patch of red on the abdomen, but this is not likely to be seen in the living bird, which presents only its back to the observer as it seeks its insect quarry on the trunks and boughs of trees. In the lower plumage the white predominates; the lower back is white, as are the sides of the head and neck. The shoulders, upper back, wings, and tail are black speckled with white.

Its habits are those of the woodpecker family. It moves about in a jerky manner, like a mechanical toy. Its method is to start low down on the trunk of a tree and work upwards, searching for insects. Unlike the nut-hatch, the woodpecker seems to object to working head downwards, so that, when it reaches the top of the tree, it flies off to another. Its movements in the air are as jerky as those on the tree-trunk.

While other birds are hunting for insects that fly in the air, or creep on the ground, or lurk under the leaves of trees, the woodpecker has designs on those that burrow into tree-trunks or hide in the crevices of the bark. These the woodpecker evicts by means of its bill and tongue. The former is stout and square at the end, which presents a chisel-like edge. The bird is thereby enabled to cut holes in the hardest wood. Occasionally it literally excavates its quarry, but, as a rule, it is not obliged to resort to such drastic measures. A series of vigorous taps on the bark under which insects are lurking usually frightens them to such an extent that they bolt from their hiding-places as hastily as men leave their habitations during an earthquake. When the insects expose themselves the woodpecker's tongue comes into operation. This organ is a fly-paper of the most approved "catch-'em-alive-o" type. It is covered with a secretion as sticky as birdlime. The insects it touches adhere to it, one and all are drawn into the woodpecker's mouth, and forthwith gathered unto their fathers!

The nest is of the usual woodpecker type, that is to say, a cavity in the trunk or a thick branch of a tree, partially, at any rate, excavated by the bird. Although the chisel-like bill of the woodpecker can cut the hardest wood, the bird usually selects for the site of its nest a part of the tree where the internal wood is rotten. This, of course, means less work for the bird. The only hard labour it has then to perform is to cut through the sound external wood a neat, round passage leading to the decayed core. When once this is reached, little further effort is required.

Last year I spent a few days at Easter in the Himalayas, and there had leisure to watch a pair of pied woodpeckers at work on their nest. These birds were brown-fronted pied woodpeckers—*Dendrocopus auriceps*. Their nest was being excavated in the trunk of a large rhododendron tree, at a spot some thirty feet from the ground. When I first began to watch the birds the cock was at work. He confined his operations to a spot about four inches from the surface, so that, as he hammered away, his head, neck, and a part of his shoulders disappeared in the hole. His fore toes grasped the inside of the aperture, and his hind toes the bark of the tree. The wood at which he was working was sufficiently hard to cause the taps of his bill to ring out clearly. After I had been watching him for about ten minutes he flew off to a tree hard by and uttered a number of curious low notes. Then his spouse appeared and he caressed her. After this both birds flew off. A few seconds later the hen came to the nest hole and set to work. Her efforts were not directed to the part of the cavity at which the cock had been working. Her taps were at a spot deeper down, so that while at work her tail, although at right angles to her body, derived no support from the trunk. She was operating on soft wood, hence the tapping of her bill was scarcely audible. After working for about eight minutes she began to remove the chips of wood she had detached. This operation is performed so rapidly that it is apt to be overlooked. The bird plunges its head into the hollow, seizes some chips, draws out its head and jerks this violently to one side, usually to the right, and thus casts the chips over its shoulder.

After the hen had been at work for nearly ten minutes she flew away. Within one minute and a half of her departure the cock arrived on the scene, and at once set to work in a most business-like fashion. He now operated on the right side of the cavity, and not at the spot to which his wife had directed her attention. After working for exactly twenty-five minutes the cock flew off. Then for a fraction over ten minutes the hole was deserted. At the end of this time it was the cock who again appeared. He put in a spell of thirty-five minutes' work, in the course of which he indulged in a "breather" lasting three minutes. I then went away, and returned nearly three hours later, by which time the work had advanced to such an extent that when a bird was excavating at the deepest part of the cavity only the tail and the tip of the wing were visible. I found that the habit of the birds was to cease working about 4 p.m. I do not know at what hour they commenced work.

Five days later the nest hole had attained such a size that the birds were able to turn round in it, and so now emerged head foremost. When throwing away the chips, the head of the bird would appear at the aperture with the beak full of chips and dispose of them with a jerk of the head. The head of a woodpecker at the entrance to its hole is a pretty sight, so bright and keen is its eye. The excavation of the nest from start to finish probably occupies from ten to fourteen days.

The yellow-fronted pied woodpecker sometimes selects as a nesting site a spot in a tree-trunk only a few inches above the level of the ground.

Some years ago my ignorance of this fact afforded me a rather amusing experience. I noticed a pied woodpecker with some insects in its bill. Obviously it was about to carry these to its young. As there was only one clump of about six trees in the vicinity the nest was necessarily in one of these. Having half an hour to spare, I determined to wait and discover the whereabouts of the nest. The sun was powerful, so I elected to squat in the shade close by the trunk of the smallest of the trees. I anticipated that the woodpecker would fly direct to its nest with the food. Birds that nest in holes are usually quite indifferent to the presence of man; instinct teaches them that their nest is in an inaccessible place. But, in this instance, the bird kept hopping about looking very distressed. Consequently, I came to the conclusion that its nest must be in the trunk of the tree near which I was crouching. I stood up and examined the trunk carefully, but found no signs of a nest. I again sat down and waited until the patience of the woodpecker should be exhausted, but it continued to hop about on a log of wood with the food in its beak and disgust plainly depicted in its face. At the end of half an hour I went off mystified. The following day I returned to the spot, and the first thing that caught my eye was the entrance to the woodpecker's nest eight inches off the ground in the trunk by which I had sat on the previous day. I had then unwittingly been blocking the approach of the bird!

VII

A JHIL OUT OF SEASON

EVEN as every English seaside resort has its "season," so is there for every Indian *jhil* a period of the year when it is thronged with avian visitors. At other times of the year the *jhil*, like the seaside town, is, comparatively speaking, deserted. The season of the *jhil* extends from October to April—a term long enough to turn the average lodging-house keeper green with envy! During the winter months the *jhils* of Northern India are full to overflowing with ducks, geese, coots, pelicans, cormorants, and waders of every length of leg. As the weather grows hot, the majority of these take to their wings and hie themselves to cooler climes, where they enter upon the joyous toil of rearing up their families. Thus, from May to September, the permanent residents hold undisputed possession of the *jhil*. The number of these permanent residents is considerable, so that a *jhil*, even in the rains, when it contains most water, has not the forlorn appearance of, let us say, Margate in winter.

It is very pleasant during a short break in the rains to visit a *jhil* late in the afternoon, especially if a breeze be blowing. The sky presents a panorama of clouds of the most varied and fantastic shapes, to which the setting sun imparts hues wonderful and beautiful. The slanting rays are reflected and refracted from cloud to cloud, so that not infrequently there appear to be two suns behind the clouds, a major one setting in the west and a minor one sinking to the eastern horizon. The earth below is very beautiful. It is clothed in a mantle of green of every hue, from the vivid emerald of the young rice crop to the dark bluish green of the pipal tree. As likely as not the *jhil* is so thickly studded with grasses and other aquatic plants as to present the appearance, from a little distance, of a number of flooded fields, in most of which are well-grown crops—the water being visible only in patches here and there.

The most conspicuous of the occupants of the *jhil* are the snow-white egrets (*Herodias alba*). These birds, which attain a length of a yard, strut about solemnly in the shallower parts of the lake, seeking their quarry. Their long necks project high above the vegetation; so slender are these that they might almost belong to swans. Here and there stands motionless a "long-necked heron, dread of nimble eels" (*Ardea cinerea*), waiting patiently until a luckless frog shall approach. The grey plumage of this species, dull and sober though it be, stands out in bold contrast to the surrounding greenery. In another part of the *jhil* a couple of sarus cranes (*Grus antigone*) are visible. This is the only species of crane resident in India; the others are to be numbered among those which visit the *jhil* in the "season." One of the saruses, like the heroine of the "penny dreadful," has drawn himself up to his full height, and his grey form, relieved by patches of red and white on the head and neck, shows well against the background of dark foliage. His mate is apparently sitting down. This probably indicates the presence of a nest. To discover this we must wade and chance an occasional immersion to the waist. Risking this, we advance, to the disgust of the saruses, who set up a loud trumpeting. Sometimes the parent birds attack the intruders. Such conduct is, however, rare. Usually the sarus indulges in Lloyd-Georgian methods of meeting an enemy.

The nest in question is a pile of rushes and water-weeds, rising a couple of feet from the water and large enough for a man to stand upon. It contains two whitish eggs faintly blotched with yellowish brown.

Viewed from the margin, the *jhil* appears to be utterly devoid of waterfowl; but in this case things are not what they seem. Before we have waded far in the direction of the nest of the sarus, numbers of duck and teal which were hidden by the sedges and grasses get up and fly to another part of the *jhil*.. The first birds to be disturbed are some cotton-teal (*Nettopus coromandelianus*). As these consist of a flock of eight or ten they are obviously not nesting. The cotton-teal drake is a bird easy to identify. Its small size, white head, and black necklace are unmistakable, and the white margins to the wings are very conspicuous during flight.

On another part of the *jhil* a pair of spot-billed ducks (*Anas poecilorhyncha*) settle down. These are recognisable even at a considerable distance when in the water by the white patch on each flank. As there are two of these birds together it is probable that they have a nest hidden in one of the sedge-covered islets studded about the tank. The other ducks disturbed by our approach are whistling teal (*Dendrocycna javanica*), which occur in considerable flocks, and a few comb-duck (*Sarcidiornis melanotus*). All these species of duck and teal are permanent residents in India.

Not a single coot is to be seen upon the *jhil*. The explanation of this is that this particular tank dries up in the hot weather, and coots usually keep to those lakes that contain water all the year round.

Half a dozen terns form a conspicuous and beautiful feature of the *jhil*. As they sail overhead, with every now and then a descent to the water to secure a frog or small fish, their silvery wings stand out boldly from a dark cloud on the southern horizon. The terns at the *jhil* are all of the black-bellied species (*Sterna melanogaster*). The other species haunt rivers in preference to shallow lakes.

Last, but not least, mention must be made of Pallas's fishing eagle (*Haliaetus leucoryphus*). One or more pairs of this bird are to be seen in the vicinity of every *jhil*. In the earlier part of the day they are active, screaming creatures, but when once they have made a good meal off a teal or some fish they become very sluggish. Two of them are sitting about fifty yards apart on a *band* alongside the *jhil*, looking like kites with whitish heads. They sit as motionless as statues. They are obviously feeling very lazy. Presently a king-crow (*Dicrurus ater*) comes up and, uttering that soft note which seems to be peculiar to the rainy season, makes repeated feints at the head of one of the fishing eagles. Save for a slight inclination of the head, the eagle pays no attention to the attack of its puny adversary. Eventually, the king-crow gives up in despair and flies off, probably to find something which will take more notice of his threatening demonstrations.

Even when I approach the fishing eagle the phlegmatic bird only flies a few yards. There is no creature more sluggish than a bird or beast of prey that has recently made a good meal.

VIII

BIRDS IN WHITE

ALMOST every species of bird and beast throws off an occasional albinistic variation or sport, which tends to breed true. Such sports are of two kinds—complete and incomplete albinos. In the former, the organism is totally devoid of external pigment, so that the eye looks red, there being no colouring matter in the iris to mask the small blood vessels in it. In the incomplete albinistic form the iris retains the pigment, so that the eye colour is normal. True albinos have very poor sight, hence when such sports occur in a species in a state of nature they soon perish in the struggle for existence. The white varieties with pigmented eyes are not handicapped by bad eyesight, but their whiteness makes them conspicuous to the creatures that prey upon them; so that, unless they are well able to defend themselves or unless they dwell in a region of everlasting snow, they tend to be eliminated by natural selection.

If protective colouring were as important to the welfare of birds as Wallaceians and modern Darwinians assert, all the birds of the Polar regions would be white and not a single white species would be found in the temperate zones or in the Tropics. That coloured species occur in the Arctic regions and white species in the Tropics is conclusive proof that in those particular cases, at any rate, it is not of paramount importance to the species that they be protectively coloured.

Finn and I have shown in *The Making of Species* that the ice-bound Arctic and Antarctic regions are not inhabited, as popular works on zoology would have us believe, by a snow-white fauna. We have shown that in the Polar countries the coloured species of birds outnumber the white species. I will, therefore, not dilate further upon this subject. It will suffice to repeat that in the area of eternal snow the white forms are at an advantage in the struggle for existence, as their whiteness tends to render them difficult to see, while, in regions where snow is unknown, such organisms labour under a disadvantage because of their conspicuousness, and, other things being equal, they ought not to be able to hold their own against less showy rivals.

The fact that white birds exist in the plains of India must mean that their colour is not a matter of great importance, that a conspicuous organism can survive in the fight for life provided it be otherwise well equipped for the contest. From this it follows that it is incorrect to speak of the whiteness of such organisms as the direct product of natural selection.

Let us take a brief survey of those birds of India of which the plumage is largely white, and try to discover how it is that each of them is able to hold its own in the struggle for existence, notwithstanding its showy plumage. These birds are the spoonbill, the egrets, the black-winged stilt, the avocet, the white ibis, the flamingo, adult cock paradise flycatcher, and certain of the gulls, terns, pelicans and storks, including the open-bill. With many of these every one is familiar. Accordingly, it will not be necessary to describe the sea gulls, the pelicans or the flamingo.

The spoonbill (*Platalea leucorodia*) is a bird larger than a kite with very long black legs and a bill of the same hue which is flat and expanded at the end like a spoon, hence the popular name of the bird. Perhaps another name for the bird—Banjo-bill—still better describes its beak. Spoonbills dwell on the fringe of water and feed much as ducks do.

The white ibis (*Ibis melanocephala*) is another wading bird, rather smaller than the spoonbill and with considerably shorter legs. All its plumage is white, but the legs, bill, and featherless head and upper neck are black. The bill is long and curved like that of the curlew. The stilt (*Himantopus candidus*) may be described as a sandpiper on red stilts. It is a white bird with dark wings and back which spends its days wading in shallow water. The avocet (*Recurvirostra avocetta*) is perhaps the most elegant of all wading birds. It is slightly bigger than the stilt but with shorter legs. Its body is white picked out with black. Its most characteristic feature is a long, slender bill which curves upwards. Like the species already mentioned, it feeds in shallow water, and I have seen it on the Cooum.

The open-bill (*Anastomus oscitans*) looks like a shabby specimen of the common white stork. It is characterised by a peculiar beak, of which the mandibles do not meet in the middle and look as though they had been bent in an attempt to crack a hard nut. The egrets, of which there are several species in India, are snow-white, heron-like birds. The most familiar is the cattle egret (*Bubulcus coromandus*), which Finn characterises as one of the most picturesque birds in the East. This is the bird that struts along beside a cow or buffalo and seizes the grasshoppers disturbed by the motion of the quadruped. It is the least aquatic of all the egrets, most of which are true waders.

Terns may be described as very graceful and slenderly built gulls. Their feet are webbed, so that they can swim after the manner of ducks and sea gulls, but they spend most of their time on their powerful pinions and so elegant is their flight that they have been called sea-swallows. The adult cock paradise flycatcher (*Terpsiphone paradisi*) is one of the most beautiful birds in the world. As he is described in another essay it is only necessary for me to state in this place that he is a white bird with a black-crested head. He is not much larger than a sparrow, but his two median tail feathers are twenty inches in length and float behind him like streamers of white satin as he flits from tree to tree.

It will be observed that of the above list of Indian birds that are mainly white, only the paradise flycatcher belongs to the great Order of *Passeres;* moreover, with this exception, all are wading or aquatic birds. These are significant facts if we can interpret them aright. I interpret them in the following manner. It may be taken as a fact that every species throws off occasionally white mutations or sports, which breed true, so that, if allowed to persist, they form the starting point for new varieties and species. As most passerine birds are small and preyed upon by the *raptores*, white varieties among them usually perish at an early age on account of their conspicuousness. Thus there are very few white passerine birds. The paradise flycatcher lives amid thick foliage, and so is comparatively immune from the attacks of birds of prey ; but even here it is noteworthy that the hens are not white but chestnut in colour throughout life, and the cocks have chestnut-coloured plumage until they are two years old. As the cock shares in the duties of incubation equally with the hen, her failure to acquire white plumage cannot be accounted for by supposing her to have a greater need of protection. Finn has suggested that the whiteness of the cock is a senile character ; that it is the livery of old age.

The majority of the non-passerine birds that are altogether or mainly white are large and able to fight well, so that they are comparatively immune from the attacks of raptorial birds. The gulls and terns, although small, fly so powerfully as to be equally safe. In the case of birds which secure their food in the water, whiteness is probably useful in rendering them less conspicuous to organisms living in the liquid medium than they would be were they coloured.

Further, whiteness of feather seems to be correlated in some way with the power to resist cold and damp.

It should be noted that not one of the larger fruit-eating birds is white. The reason of this would seem to be that in the case of non-aquatic birds such white species possess no advantage in the struggle for existence, but, on the contrary, the whiteness of their plumage is perhaps correlated with weakness of constitution. This, of course, is a heavier handicap to a large bird than being conspicuous is.

The correlation or interdependence of various characteristics and organs is a subject full of interest, but one which has hitherto attracted comparatively little attention. Close study of this phenomenon may eventually revolutionise zoological thought. Whether this surmise prove right or wrong, one thing is certain, and that is there is more in the philosophy of whiteness than the old-fashioned evolutionist dreams of.

IX

THE PIED CRESTED CUCKOO

THE pied crested cuckoo (*Coccystes jacobinus*) is the most handsome of all the cuckoos. He is more than this. He stands out head and shoulders above his fellow-deceivers. Lest these words should convey an exaggerated idea of his splendour, let me say that they do not necessarily mean very much. Among the family of parasitic cuckoos the standard of beauty is not high. Most of the *Cuculidæ* not only lack bright colours, ornamental plumes, and other superfluous appendages, but are also devoid of the smart appearance and soldier-like bearing that characterise the great majority of the feathered folk. Thus it cometh to pass that the pied crested cuckoo, although he cannot hold a candle to such birds as the paradise flycatcher or the oriole, is able to point the claw of scorn at his fellow-cuckoos. His black-and-white livery is distinctly stylish and is embellished by a crest that does not lie down as though it were ashamed of itself, but projects prettily from the back of the head.

Even as a little girl of my acquaintance calls every plump Indian a Bengali, so do the inhabitants of

Bengal call all birds possessing these pretty crests bulbuls. On this principle the Bengali name for the pied crested cuckoo is *Kola bulbul*. On the other hand, black bulbuls (*Hypsipetes*), which possess no crests, are not recognised as bulbuls by the natives of India. Obviously, the crest maketh the bulbul.

The pied crested cuckoo is a bird that is easily recognised. The upper parts of his plumage are black, his lower parts and the tips of his tail feathers are white. There is in each wing a conspicuous white bar. Then, there is the black crest. As regards size the plumage of the common cuckoo would fit our pied crested friend like a glove.

But it is not necessary to set eyes on him in order to recognise him. To hear him sufficeth. In this respect he differs in no way from his brother cuckoos. A silent cuckoo is unthinkable. The generating of sound is to the cuckoo what wine is to the wine-bibber, poker to the gambler, fighting to the soldier, "votes for women" to the Suffragette. According to cuculine philosophy, life without noise is but the image of death. The reason of this is obvious. At the breeding season a vast amount of surplus energy is generated in birds. This has to find some outlet. It is usually dissipated in the form of vocal effort, the dances and antics of courtship, and the labours of nest building and feeding the young. Or it may find expression in more concrete form in the growth of plumes and other ornaments. To the parasitic cuckoos most of these outlets are closed. They do not produce nuptial ornaments; to build nests they know not how. They are denied the pleasurable labours of rearing up their offspring. They do not appear to indulge in elaborate courtship. All their superfluous energy is sent forth in the form of noise. Watch any cuckoo while he is calling, be it the cheery *canorus*, who gladdens the Himalayas, or the koel or the brain-fever bird or the pied crested cuckoo, who enliven the plains, and you will be driven to the conclusion that they are demented creatures. Although the frenzied screaming of the pied cuckoo is easily recognised, it is difficult to describe. "Its call," writes Stuart Baker, "is a very loud metallic double note, too harsh to be called a whistle. In the early part of the season, before its voice has fully formed, its cries are particularly harsh and disagreeable, and the second note, which should be the same in tone as the first, often goes off at a tangent. Later on in the year, though it becomes more noisy than ever, its notes are rather musical."

Much remains to be discovered regarding the distribution of the pied crested cuckoo in India. Although it has been observed in most parts of the country, it appears to undergo considerable local migration. In Northern India I have seen the bird only during the rains, but I believe that there are cases on record of its occurring there in winter. On the other hand, I have seen pied crested cuckoos in Madras in July, at which time they are supposed all to migrate northwards. An anonymous writer recently put forward the theory that our Indian cuckoos are not really migratory, that they appear to migrate because of their skulking habits. Cuckoos are loved by their fellow-birds about as much as Lord Morley is loved by Anglo-Indians. As cuckoos dislike demonstrations, the theory is that they habitually shun observation, and are therefore not noticed, except at the breeding season, when their loud excited calls betray their presence. This theory is a plausible one, but the facts are, I think, against it. There can be no doubt that some species of cuckoo are migratory. Indeed, one of the earlier theories to account for the parasitic habits of the common cuckoo was that the bird did not stay in England sufficiently long to enable it to rear up a brood. Again, the Indian koel (*Eudynamis honorata*) certainly migrates. No bird is commoner in Lahore in the hot weather, but I did not set eyes upon the bird there in the course of two winters during which I took several walks a week, armed with field-glasses. Likewise the pied crested cuckoo is also migratory, but the particular direction of its movements remains to be established. I would ask every one interested in birds to make a note of each date on which this cuckoo is seen.

The parasitic habits of the pied cuckoo are interesting. The bird victimises various species of babbler, more especially the jungle babbler (*Crateropus canorus*) and the large grey babbler (*Argya malcomi*). There is nothing particularly remarkable in this, for babblers are the favourite dupes of Indian cuckoos. The point that is of interest is that the common hawk-cuckoo, or brain-fever bird (*Hierococcyx varius*) also victimises the seven sisters. Now this cuckoo is much like a hawk in appearance, so much so that it affords the stock example of aggressive mimicry among birds. Says the Wallaceian: "This cuckoo resembles a hawk so closely that small birds mistake it for one. When the nesting babblers see it, they flee for their lives, and the cuckoo—the ass in the lion's skin—seizes the opportunity to deposit an egg in the momentarily deserted nest. The strange egg is not noticed by the babblers on their return because it is blue like theirs. We thus see how natural selection has brought about the hawk-like appearance of the brain-fever bird, and caused the egg to become blue." If all cuckoos parasitic on babblers were like hawks in appearance, I should have nothing to urge against the above explanation. Unfortunately for the Wallaceians, the pied crested and other cuckoos, which do not look in the least like hawks, successfully dupe the seven sisters. It would seem, therefore, that this elaborate disguise of the hawk-cuckoo is quite unnecessary. I grant that it may make very smooth the path of the brain-fever bird. This, however, is not enough. As I have repeatedly said, almost I fear *ad nauseam*, natural selection cannot be said to have brought about a structural peculiarity which is proved to be merely useful, and not essential. Unless it can be shown that, but for a certain peculiarity, a species would have perished, it is incorrect to speak of natural selection as having fixed that characteristic in the species by eliminating all individuals that did not possess it. Moreover, if it can be shown that any specified character has such a survival value, the selectionist has still to prove that the characteristic had this value at the earliest, and at each successive stage of its development.

I submit, then, that the Wallaceian's explanation of the hawk-like appearance of the brain-fever bird is in all probability not the correct one. In the same way it is doubtful whether the blue eggs of the brain-fever bird and the pied crested cuckoo can be fairly laid to the charge of natural selection. The common cuckoo sometimes lays its eggs, which are not blue, in the nests of birds whose eggs are blue, for example the hedge-sparrow in England and the Himalayan laughing thrush in India.

The pied crested cuckoo, when it first leaves the nest, differs considerably from the adult in appearance. Its upper parts are slaty grey, and its lower parts, the wing patch and the tips of the outer tail feathers are pale buff, so that the young cuckoo, when flying, might easily be mistaken for a bank myna (*Acridotheres ginginianus*) but for the length of its tail. Like all young cuckoos, it is a greedy, querulous thing. It sits on a branch, clamouring continually for food, flapping its wings and uttering a very fair imitation of the babbler call.

September is the month in which to look out for young pied cuckoos. Those that I have seen appear always to be unaccompanied by foster-brothers or sisters. This would seem to indicate either that the parent cuckoos destroy the legitimate eggs at the time of depositing their own, or that the young birds have the depraved habits of the youthful *Cuculus canorus*.

But there are cases on record of young pied crested cuckoos being accompanied by young babblers. It is thus evident that much remains to be discovered regarding the habits of *Coccystes jacobinus*.

X

VULTURES

HAVING dealt in *Bombay Ducks* with what I may perhaps term the domestic vulture of India—*Neophron ginginianus*, or Pharaoh's chicken—I do not propose again to discuss this worthy but ugly fowl. Nevertheless, before passing on to the aristocratic vultures, I cannot resist the temptation to reproduce Phil Robinson's inimitable description of our familiar *Neophron:* "A shabby-looking fowl of dirty white plumage, about the size of an able-bodied hen, but disproportionately long for its height, pacing seriously along the high road, taking each step with its legs set wide apart, with all the circumspection of a Chinaman among papers, but keeping its eyes as busily about it for chance morsels of refuse as any other professional scavenger. The traffic, both of vehicles and foot passengers, may be considerable, but the vulture is a municipal institution and knows it. No one thinks of molesting it; indeed, if it chose to obstruct the footpath, the natives would make way for it. Children let it alone, and dogs do not run after it. So it goes plodding through its day's work, solemn, and shabby, and hungry, uncomplaining, and poor, and at night flaps up into some tree and quietly dozes off to sleep." *Neophron ginginianus* always puts me in mind of the heroes in some of George Gissing's novels.

Very different are the ways of the other members of the vulture tribe. They are not content to wander about among rubbish heaps and in other still less savoury places in the hope of securing any small morsel. They demand substantial fare; nothing less than a large carcase pleases them. It is true that they have sometimes to put up with garbage of the lesser sort, so that those which have not been successful in their hunt have perforce to gather in the trees near the municipal slaughter-house and await the casting forth of the offal. Their usual method of securing a meal is of the won-by-waiting description. They mount high into the air and float on outstretched pinions 3000 or 4000 feet or more above the level of the earth, and thence scan its surface with eager eye. When the hand of death strikes any terrestrial creature, down comes the soaring vulture. His earthward flight is observed by his neighbour, floating in the air a mile away, who follows quickly after number one. In a few seconds numbers three, four, five, six, and others are also making for the quarry, so that the stricken creature, before life has left it, is surrounded by a crowd of hungry vultures, and, as the poet has it, "but lives to feel the vultures bick'ring for their horrid meal." Nor do these wait for death to set in before they begin their ghastly repast. It suffices that their wretched victim is too feeble to harm them; they then set to work to tear it to pieces, utterly indifferent to its cries of agony. Such behaviour is characteristic of all birds and beasts of prey. These, in consequence, have been dubbed "cruel" by those who should know better. Thus Bonner, in his "Forest Creatures," writes: "Just as a child likes to enjoy the consciousness of having possession of a cake, and revels for a while in the pleasurable feeling before taking the first bite, feeling sure that delay will not weaken his tenure, so will an eagle very often toy with his victim, and though within his grasp, defer the fatal grip. At such times his appetite is probably not very keen; or he is in a merry humour and likes the fun of seeing the terror he causes, as he races in his mirth round and round the animal almost paralysed with fear. Or perhaps there is somewhat of a Caligula in his nature, and he considers *that* the only true enjoyment which is purchased by the acute suffering of others. Be this as it may, he will thus dally with a creature's anguish, and only after having twenty times swooped down as if to seize it in his talons, do so in reality."

To call such behaviour on the part of a bird of prey cruel is, I submit, utterly wrong, and based on an altogether incorrect perception of the animal mind. It is my belief that vultures and other raptorial birds do not recognise in the screams of their victims the wails of pain. Their power of reasoning is not sufficient to enable them to interpret the meaning of these cries. How can they possibly know that they are hurting their victim, or that it can feel? They have never been taught that it is most painful to be torn to pieces, and they themselves have not experienced the sensation. How, then, are they to understand that it hurts? An Indian coolie, even, does not appear to appreciate the fact that birds can feel pain, for when accompanying a man out shooting he will pick up a winged snipe or duck and put it, while still alive, in the game stick and leave it there to die a lingering death. Now, I readily admit that the Indian villager is not overburdened with brains, but he is capable of simple reasoning, which is more than can be said of any bird. He certainly is not conscious that by putting the head of a live bird into a game stick he is causing unnecessary pain; much more are birds of prey ignorant of the fact that being eaten alive is a most painful experience.

A crowd of vultures gathers round a stricken animal in almost as short a space of time as a mob of gaping Londoners collects round the victim of an accident. Recently, in the course of a shoot in the Terai, the man in the *machan* next to mine shot a spotted deer, which fell lifeless in an open patch in the forest. By the time the line of beaters had reached our *machans* fifteen or sixteen vultures had assembled round the dead stag, and it was with difficulty that we, from our *machans*, kept the greedy birds off the carcase.

Vultures are always to be found at the burning *ghat*. Wood is expensive in many parts of India, so that only the more wealthy completely burn the remains of their dead relatives. For the poor and the parsimonious the vultures complete the work commenced by the fire, so that truer than even its author suspected is Michelet's description of vultures as "beneficent crucibles of living fire through which Nature passes everything that might corrupt the higher life." When a body, with the face only singed, is cast on to the Ganges, at least one vulture alights upon it and proceeds to devour it as it is borne on the waters of the sacred river; the air and gases in the corpse keep both it and the vulture afloat. Sooner or later a rent causes the gases to escape, then the corpse sinks suddenly and the vulture is often hard put to it to reach the bank, for it cannot fly properly when its wings are wet. The half-burnt corpse is not always consigned to the river, and in these circumstances the scene at the *ghat* when the living human beings have left it is not one that is pleasant to contemplate. But in India, where Nature's back premises are so exposed, it is not always possible to avoid it. More than once when strolling along a river bank have I suddenly and unexpectedly come upon a company of vultures squatting in an irregular circle round some object, each fighting with its neighbour for a place at the repast. The vultures are not the only participants. Some pariah dogs run about on the outskirts, every now and then making frantic efforts to wedge themselves in between the vultures and so obtain for their emaciated bodies a mouthful of food. Some crows and kites are invariably present, trusting to their superior agility to snatch an occasional morsel. And in the Punjab some ravens will also be at the feast.

There are several species of vulture in India. Next to the scavenger vulture the commonest is the white-backed species (*Pseudogyps bengalensis*). This is not a bad-looking bird in its solemn lugubrious way. Its general colour is ashy black—the black of a threadbare coat. Its back is white, but this is usually nearly entirely hidden by the dark wings, and shows merely as a thin streak of white along the middle of the back. The dark grey head and neck are almost devoid of feathers and their nakedness is accentuated by a ruff or collar of whitish feathers. The bareness of the head makes the large hooked beak look longer and bigger than it really is. The bird is nearly a yard in length.

A yet finer bird is the black, King, or Pondicherry vulture (*Otogyps calvus*). The back and wings of this species are glossy black relieved by white patches on the thighs. Its bare head and neck are yellowish red, and there is a wattle of this colour on each side of the head. This vulture, unlike the last species, is solitary, and is called the "King vulture" because, when it comes to a carcase, all the vulgar herd of smaller vultures, kites, and crows give way before it, and, as a rule, are afraid to approach until this regal bird has had its fill.

Vultures build huge platforms of nests high up in lofty trees, and, like sand martins, rear up their young in the winter.

XI

THE INDIAN ROBIN

SPEAKING generally, the birds of India are to the feathered folk of the British Isles as wine is to water. The birds, such as the blue tits, which we looked upon in our youth as possessing gay plumage, seem to have lost some of their lustre when we again set eyes upon them after a sojourn in the East. It is not that they or we have grown older, that their feathers have lost their ancient splendour or that the rose rims to our spectacles have worn away. The explanation lies in the fact that we have for years been looking upon allied species of brighter hue. The English robin, however, is one of the few exceptions to this rule. He is in all respects superior to his Indian cousins—the Thamnobias. I mean no offence to the latter, for they are charming little birds, nevertheless they must bow to the superiority of their English brethren. The Indian robins lack the red waistcoat that gives the British bird his well-to-do, homely appearance. It is true that our Indian robins wear a patch of red feathers under the tail. But this, notwithstanding the fact that they make unceasing efforts to display it, is not adequate compensation for the lack of the red waistcoat. It is not so much what one wears as the way in which one wears things that matters. To wear brown boots with light-coloured clothes is no offence against good taste, although at one time the undergraduates at Pembroke College, Cambridge, were not allowed to wear brown boots in chapel; but to don this description of footwear simultaneously with a frock coat is a sin that is likely to be visited upon the children—I was about to say—unto the fourth generation, but in this horrid, democratic, Lloyd-Georgian age I think it would be more correct to say "unto the second generation." Nor is this the only point of inferiority of the Indian robin. Although he is by no means a poor singer, he is not nearly so brilliant a performer as his British cousin.

Then again, the Indian robin has not the confidential manners of the English species. Often when I have been sitting in an English garden, has a robin come and perched on the arm of my chair, an example which his Indian counterpart has never shown the slightest inclination to follow. In England the robin is a semi-domesticated bird; in India, although a pair often take up their abode in the compound, robins prefer to dwell "far from the madding crowd." If the truth must be told the Indian species love not the shady garden. The cool orchard has no attractions for them. They abhor the babbling brook. Their idea of an earthly paradise is a brick-kiln, a railway embankment, or a flat, rocky, barren, arid piece of land. Aloes and prickly pear are their favourite plants.

But enough of these odious comparisons. Let me now describe the two Indian species of Thamnobia—the black-backed robin (*T. fulicata*) which has possessed itself of South India and the brown-backed species (*T. cambayensis*) which is found all over Northern India. The cock of the former species is a glossy, jet-black bird, with a narrow white bar in his wing, and the brick-red patch under his tail which I have already had occasion to mention. The hen is sandy brown all over save for the aforesaid patch. The hen of the northern species differs in no appreciable way from her sister in the South; while the cock of the North varies only from his southern brother in having the back brown instead of black. It is my belief that the black-backed species arose as a mutation from the brown-backed form. The hen and the two cocks probably represent three stages in the evolutionary process.

I am sorry to be under the necessity of making a statement which may offend the ladies, but the fact is that among birds the cocks tend to be ahead of the hens as regards evolutionary development, they are, in a sense, superior beings. The tendency is for all birds to assume brilliant plumage, and it is fitting that this should be so, for are not birds the most exquisite ornaments of the earth? In some species both sexes have travelled equally far along the evolutionary path, and in such instances the sexes are alike. In other cases one of the sexes is one or more stages ahead of the other, and it is almost invariably the cock who leads and who is, therefore, the more beautiful. It is my belief that at one time both sexes of both species of Indian robin were coloured as the hens now are. Later, a mutation arose in the cock whereby all his plumage save the back became black, and when this mutation became fixed in the species, the cock had advanced a stage in his evolutionary progress. A still more advanced stage was reached when the whole of the plumage became black. Could we peep a thousand years into the future, it is quite likely that we should find that the northern species of Indian robin had acquired a black back.

Some may think that these statements are far-fetched. I submit that they are nothing of the kind. Not infrequently it happens that hen birds develop the plumage of the male. Again, sometimes of two closely allied species one displays marked sexual differences, while the sexes of the other are difficult to distinguish. Every one is familiar with the showy drake and the dull-coloured hen of the common mallard or wild duck of Europe (*Anas boscas*), and we in India are equally familiar with an allied species the spotted bill (*A. poecilorhyncha*), in which both sexes are dull-coloured like the female mallard. The cock mallard is a stage ahead of the hen mallard and of both sexes of the spotted bill as regards evolutionary development. A thousand years hence the male spotted-bill may have developed a coat of many colours. The foregoing will not be acceptable to the old-fashioned Darwinians, but as these cannot explain satisfactorily how it is that natural selection has given cock robin in Northern India a brown back, and a black back to his southern cousin, they are not entitled to dictate to us. The Darwin-Wallace hypothesis has been of great service to Science during the past fifty years, but zoology has now outgrown it, and sooner or later all scientific men must recognise this fact. But we have made a long digression into the arid field of science, let us hie back to our Indian robins.

Perhaps their most interesting characteristic is their fondness for queer nesting sites. There is nothing particularly remarkable about the nest itself, which varies according to its situation, from a mere pad to a neat cup composed of soft materials, such as cotton, grass, and vegetable fibres. The nursery is cosily lined, frequently with feathers. The lining almost invariably contains some human or horse hair, and often fragments of snake's skin. In April and May of one year I came upon the following robins' nests at Lahore: No. 1, in the disused nest of a rat-bird (*Argya caudata*) placed about five feet above the ground in a thorny but dense bush; No. 2, on the outer sill of a window, which was guarded by trellis-work, the meshes of which were so fine that it was with difficulty that I could insert two fingers into the nest; No. 3, in a hole in the mud wall of a deserted hut; No. 4, among the roots of a sago palm tree; No. 5, in a very dilapidated disused rat-bird's nest; No. 6, in a hole in a railway embankment; No. 7, in a hole barely a foot from the ground in the trunk of a tree—in the same hole was a wasps' nest; No. 8, in one of the spaces between bricks that had been stacked in order to become dried by the sun.

The above form a varied assortment of sites; but there is nothing very remarkable in any of them. Colonel Marshall records a nest built in the hole in a wall intended for the passage of a punkah rope.

At Fategarh, some years ago, a pair of robins built inside an old watering pot that had been thrown into a bush. Another pair went "one better" by nesting in the loop of an old piece of cloth that had been thrown over the branch of a tree.

Mr. J. T. Fry records in *The Countryside Monthly* a nest built at Jhansi in a long-haired brush used for taking down cobwebs. "The nest," he writes, "is constructed of the fine roots of the *khus-khus* lined with hair into which onion peel and scraps of cast-off snake's skin have been incorporated. The brush, when out of use, was placed against the wall at the side of the bungalow, being fixed to the end of a long bamboo. It was only in use about a fortnight before the nest was discovered."

The above were all nests of the brown-backed robin, but the black-backed species selects equally curious nesting sites. As examples of these mention may be made of holes in railway cuttings within a few feet of the line, holes in walls, the side of a haystack, a hole in a gatepost. Dr. Blanford found the nest of this species inside the bamboo of a *dhooly* in the verandah of Captain Glasfurd's house at Sironcha. Mr. J. Macpherson records a nest in an elephant's skull lying out in his compound at Mysore.

Both sexes take part in nest construction. At the mating season cock robins are very bold and pugnacious, but these characteristics do not always save the nest from destruction, as the following incident will show.

In May, 1912, a pair of brown-backed robins elected to nest in the verandah of my bungalow at Fyzabad. The roof of the verandah is supported by longitudinal beams which rest on a series of cross-beams that project from the main wall of the house and lean at their far end on the verandah pillars. The upper surface of the cross-beams affords admirable nesting sites of which the doves and mynas take full advantage. The robins in question built their nest on one of these cross-beams. No sooner had the nursery been completed than trouble began. The first intimation I received of the existence of the nest was much swearing (if I may use that expression to denote the angry cries of a little bird) on the part of cock robin, The temperature on that day was well over 100° F. in the shade, consequently I did not open the doors of the house to ascertain the cause of the robin's wrath. But the angry cries of the bird persisted, and I heard them repeatedly on the following day, so I braved the heat and went into the verandah to prospect and discovered that a myna was the object of the robin's wrath.

During the following day the language of the robin abated neither in quantity nor quality; indeed, his noise began to get on my nerves. He used to perch when giving vent to his feelings, just above the heads of the *chaprassis* who sat in the verandah awaiting orders. These men are not usually very observant, but even they noticed and grew annoyed at the robin's noise, and on several occasions I heard them flicking at the robin with a duster. During the early part of the fourth day there was comparative quiet in the verandah, and I thought that the robins and mynas had settled their differences. I was mistaken. The quiet proved to be the lull before the storm. This burst about 4 p.m. The uproar brought me to the window; from there I saw that the robin was hissing with rage at a myna who was peeping into the robin's nest. Then the cock robin flew at the myna and pecked at him. The myna, although three times the size of the robin, fled and flew from the verandah, followed by the swearing robin. A couple of minutes later cock robin returned alone. He then perched on the floor of the verandah, drew himself up to his full height, like the heroine in a penny novelette (who, by the way, appears always to slouch except when she is very angry), and stood there hissing with rage. This continued until a *chaprassi*, who was squatting in the verandah, drove the angry bird away. The next morning I found lying on the floor of the verandah the wreck of the robins' nest, and noticed that a myna was constructing a nest on the site recently occupied by that of the robin.

XII

THE SHIKRA

FALCONERS divide hawks into the long-winged and the short-winged varieties. The former stand in much the same relation to the latter as the cross-country runner does to the sprinter. The long-winged hawks have dark eyes, while in the short-winged ones the eyes are yellow or orange; hence the two classes are sometimes distinguished as dark-eyed and light-eyed hawks. The various falcons, the peregrine, the laggar, the saker, etc., come in the long-winged category. When they catch sight of their quarry, they give chase and follow it, if necessary for a long distance, till they either lose it or are able to get above it in order to strike. The short-winged hawk is content with making one pounce or dash at its quarry; if it secures it, well and good, if it fails, it does not give chase. The sparrow-hawk and the shikra are familiar examples of the short-winged hawks.

The long-winged falcons are naturally held in greatest favour by the hawker; but short-winged birds of prey are also trained. Long-winged hawks hunt in the open. Being long-distance fliers, they rely chiefly upon their power of endurance, and so naturally like plenty of room in which to operate. Short-winged hawks, on the other hand, usually hunt in wooded localities, where they are better able to surprise their victims than in the open.

After the kite, the shikra (*Astur badius*) is the commonest bird of prey in India. It is in habits and appearance very like the common sparrow-hawk (*Accipiter nisus*). So great is the resemblance between the two species that "Eha," in his *Common Birds of Bombay*, gives an excellent description of the shikra under the title of the Indian sparrow-hawk.

Although the two little hawks are so similar in appearance, ornithologists place them in different genera on account of the considerably longer legs of the sparrow-hawk proper and its heavily spotted and blotched eggs, the eggs of the shikra being white and almost entirely free from spots.

The shikra is a slightly-built bird about the same length as a pigeon; its tail is half a foot long. The upper plumage is greyish. The wings and tail are heavily barred with black. The breast is white, with large brown spots in young birds; in old birds the brown spots are replaced by a number of thin wavy, rust-coloured cross-bars. The female, as is invariably the case in birds of prey, is considerably larger than the male, she being fourteen inches in length as against his twelve and a half. But it is quite useless to attempt to recognise a shikra, or indeed any other bird of prey, from a description of its plumage. As "Eha" says: "To try to make out hawks by their colour is at the best a short road to despair. Naturalists learn to recognise them as David's watchman recognised the courier who brought tidings of the victory over Absalom: 'His running is like the running of Ahimaaz the son of Zadok.' Every bird of prey has its own character, some trick of flight, some peculiarity of attitude when at rest, something in its figure and proportions which serves to distinguish it decisively. The sparrow-hawk (shikra) flies with a few rapid strokes of the wings and then a gliding motion, and this, together with its short, rounded wings and long tail, distinguishes it from any other common bird of prey. I learn of its presence oftener by the ear than the eye. Its sharp, impatient double cry arrests attention among all other bird-voices."

The shikra has comparatively feeble claws, and so is unable to tackle any large quarry. Birds of prey strike with the claw, not with the beak, as some artists would have us believe; hence the size of the claws of any particular bird of prey affords a safe index of the magnitude of its quarry. The more formidable the claw, the larger the prey. No matter how large a raptorial bird be, if its claws are small and feeble, it feeds either upon carrion or tiny creatures.

The shikra is said to live chiefly upon lizards; but it makes no bones about taking a sparrow or other small bird, a mouse, or even a rat. In default of larger game it does not despise grasshoppers, and, when the termites swarm, it will make merry among these along with the crows and kites. I once saw a shikra pounce upon a little striped squirrel. Some crows were witnesses of the feat, and at once proceeded to attack the shikra so vehemently that it let go of the squirrel, which made good its escape. The crows, let me add, were not actuated by philanthropic motives. Their object was, not to liberate the squirrel but to make a meal of it. They were quite as disappointed as the shikra when the little rodent regained its liberty.

Natives of India frequently hawk with the shikra, setting it on to partridges, quails, and mynas. It is very easily and quickly trained. Within a week or ten days of capture its education is complete. However, hawking with a shikra is, in my opinion, very poor sport, for the shikra makes but one dash at its quarry, and at once desists if it fails to secure it. The hawker holds it in his hand and throws it like a javelin in the direction of its quarry. While waiting for its victim it is carried on the hand in the same way as a merlin is, but is never hooded. It is only the dark-eyed hawks that have to be hooded; they seem to be much more excitable than the light-eyed ones. A trained shikra is very tame and does not show any objection to being handled.

The shikra nests from April to June, building, high up in a lofty tree, a nest which can scarcely be described as a triumph of avine architecture. Hume says: "These little hawks take, I should say, a full month in preparing their nest, only putting on two or three twigs a day, which they place and replace, as if they were very particular and had a great eye for a handsome nest; whereas, after all their fuss and bother, the nest is a loose, ragged-looking affair, that no respectable crow would condescend to lay in." Three bluish-white eggs are deposited in the nest. Shikra nestlings show fight when interfered with and peck savagely at the intruder.

XIII

A FINCH OF ROSEATE HUE

THE *Fringillidæ*, or finches, constitute the most successful family of birds in the world. The crow tribe runs the finches close, but the *Corvi* are handicapped by their large size. Were the sparrow as big as the crow, man would never have allowed him to become the pest that he is. The impudent pigmy is tolerated because he is so small and insignificant.

Finches are birds of coarse build, and are characterised by a vulgar-looking beak, so that they need either fine feathers or a sweet voice to render them acceptable to man. Those finches which, like the common sparrow, lack either of these attributes are accounted mean birds of low estate. But, on the whole, Dame Nature has been kind to the finches in that she has arrayed the cocks of many species in bright colours. The showy goldfinch is a familiar instance of this, as is the canary, but the yellow colour of the latter has been induced largely by artificial selection. The wild canary is not a very beautiful bird.

Among the finches all shades of red and yellow are to be found. Brown and green are worn by some species. Blue seems to be the only colour not vouchsafed to the *Fringillidæ*.

Several of the finches have the gift of song. This being so, it is regrettable that the particular species of finch which, like the poor, is always with us should have such an execrable voice. If sparrows sang like canaries what a pleasing adjunct to London they would be!

The gross, massive beak of the finch, though not good to look upon, is of great value as a seed-husking machine. No one can have watched a canary for five minutes without observing the address with which each little seed is picked up, cracked, and the husk rejected by the joint action of tongue and mandibles.

Sixty-four species of finch occur within the limits of the Indian Empire. Of these fifteen species are known as rose-finches. Rose-finches are birds of about the size of a sparrow. The plumage of the cocks is more or less suffused with crimson, while that of the hens is dark greyish olive sometimes washed with yellow. Rose-finches are essentially birds of a cold climate; they are found in Northern Europe, Asia, and America. All the Indian species, save one, are confined to the Himalayas and the country north of those mountains. The one exception is the species known as the common rose-finch (*Carpodacus erythrinus*). This spreads itself during the winter all over the plains of India as far south as the Nilgiris. I do not remember having seen it in or about Madras, but it may sometimes visit that city. In April this rose-finch goes north to breed, a few individuals remaining in the Himalayas, where they nidificate at altitudes of 10,000 feet and upwards.

The nest is a neat cup-shaped structure made of grass with a lining of fine material. It is usually built within a yard of the ground, in a bush, or even among long grass. The eggs are blue with chocolate or purple markings, which may be sparse or numerous, and may take the form of blotches, freckles, or pencillings.

The cock rose-finch, or *Tuti*, as he is always called by the natives of India, is a handsome bird. The head and neck are dull crimson, the lower parts are rosy pink and the wings are brown. The rose-finches seen in the early part of the winter are considerably less brightly coloured than those observed after Christmas. This phenomenon is due to two causes. The one is that the bird moults in September or October and dons a new suit of clothes. These are of such excellent material that they improve by wearing! As is so often the case, the margins of the new feathers are duller than the inner portion. A bird's feathers overlap like the tiles on a roof, and they overlap to such an extent that only the margin of each feather shows. As the dull edges wear away, the brighter parts begin to show, hence the gradual transition from dullness to brightness. Further, the actual colouring of the feathers becomes intensified as the spring season approaches. But in the plains of India the cock is never seen in the full glory of his crimson tunic, because he departs to high altitudes at the breeding season.

The hen rose-finch is an olive-brown bird with a tinge of yellow and some brown streaks in her plumage.

The wing is set off by a couple of whitish wing-bars. There are also bars in the wing of the cock, but these are not well defined.

Seeing how beautiful the cock rose-finch is naturally, and how successful have been the efforts to improve the canary, it may seem strange that fanciers have not turned their attention to the rose-finch, and produced, by artificial selection, a rose-finch arrayed from head to tail in crimson lake.

The fact is all the crimson colour disappears from the plumage of a rose-finch kept in captivity. Until some means of preventing this is discovered it is hopeless to attempt to breed a crimson finch.

Rose-finches live in flocks, which consist usually of from sixteen to thirty members. These flocks appear to be made up of cocks and hens in equal numbers. The birds feed on the ground, from which they pick small seeds that have fallen. " In the extreme south," writes Jerdon of the rose-finch, " I have chiefly seen it in bamboo jungle, feeding on the seeds of bamboos on several occasions, and so much is this its habit that the Telugu name signifies 'Bamboo sparrow.' " In other parts of the country it frequents alike groves, gardens, and jungles, feeding on various seeds and grain ; also not infrequently on flower buds and young leaves. Adams states that in Kashmir it feeds much on the seeds of a cultivated vetch.

During the greater part of the year the rose-finch is a silent bird. At the breeding season, and a little before it, the cock joins in the bird chorus. Its vocal efforts are well described by Blyth as " a feeble twittering song, but soft and pleasing, being intermediate to that of the goldfinch, and that of the small redpole linnet, the call note much resembling that of a canary bird."

Rose-finches are said to be very pugnacious, and in this respect they resemble their vulgar relations the sparrows, but they differ from the latter in lacking their fearlessness of man or beast. At the least alarm a flock of rose-finches feeding on the ground scurries into the nearest tree with a loud fluttering of wings. The harsh cry of the king-crow or the shadow of a passing kite is quite sufficient to cause the instant disappearance of the little flock into the foliage.

On an average, a feeding flock thus takes alarm at least twenty times in the course of an hour. Sometimes the birds take fright for no apparent reason whatever. Their behaviour in this respect is exactly like that of chaffinches, greenfinches, etc., in England, which Edmund Selous describes so accurately in that perfect nature book *Bird Watching*. Selous "came to the conclusion that the cause of flight was almost always a nervous apprehension, such as actuates schoolboys when they are doing something of a forbidden nature and half expect to see the master appear at any moment round the corner. Though there might be no discernible ground for apprehension, yet after some three or four minutes it seemed to strike the assembly that it *could* not be quite safe to remain any longer, and, presto! they were gone."

It is my belief that what may be called the undue nervousness of little birds has been caused by the attacks of birds of prey. It must as a rule be the bolder spirits—those that refuse to take refuge in the foliage at every alarm—that fall victims to the sparrow-hawk. The more nervous ones escape and transmit their innate nervousness to their offspring. There has thus arisen a race of little birds as nervous as horses.

Before a minute has passed the rose-finches, who have taken refuge in a tree, perceive that there was no ground for alarm. They then drop to the ground in twos and threes, so that, although the birds begin to return almost as soon as they have fled into the foliage, some little time elapses before the whole of the flock is again seeking food on the ground. The re-formation of a flock is a pretty sight—a shower of little birds falling from a tree like leaves in autumn.

XIV

BIRDS ON THE LAWN

IN some parts of India the hot-weather nights are sufficiently cool to allow the European inhabitants to dispense with punkas and to enjoy refreshing sleep in the open beneath the starlit sky. He who spends the night under such conditions sees and hears much of the birds. Not an hour passes in which the stillness of the darkness is not broken by the voice of some owl or cuckoo. Most of our Indian cuckoos are as nocturnal as owls. The brain-fever bird (*Hierococcyx varius*)—most vociferous of the cuculine tribe—seems to require no sleep.

The human sleeper, no matter how early he wakes in the morning, finds that some of the feathered folk have already begun the day. Every diurnal bird is up and about long before the rising of the sun. In the daylight the gauze curtains which kept the mosquitoes at bay during the night, form a most convenient cache from which to observe the doings of the birds. Birds do not see through the meshes of the mosquito nets. Eyesight is largely a matter of training. This explains why the vision of birds is so keen in some respects and so defective in others. A bird of prey while floating in the air does not fail to notice a small animal on the ground 3000 feet below. Nevertheless, that same bird will allow itself to become entangled in a coarse net stretched out in front of a tethered bird. I once asked a falconer how he would explain such inconsistencies in the behaviour of raptorial birds. He replied that in his opinion the bird of prey sees the net but fails to appreciate its nature, that the falcon looks upon the net spread before its quarry as a spider's web, as a gossamer structure that can be contemptuously swept aside. I think that the falconer's explanation is not the correct one. I believe that the bird of prey really does not see the net. It has eyes only for its quarry. It is not trained to look out for snares, having no experience of them under natural conditions. A bird that had several times been snared while stooping at its prey would learn the nature of a net and avoid it.

Similarly, birds, being unaccustomed to see living creatures emerge from apparently solid structures, do not look for human beings inside mosquito nets, and so fail to observe them. The consequence is that the birds hop and strut about the lawn within a few feet of my bed, or even perch on the mosquito curtain frame, utterly unconscious of my presence.

There is to me something very fascinating in thus watching at close quarters the ways of my feathered friends. My compound boasts of a lawn, sufficiently large for three tennis courts, which owing to much watering, mowing, and rolling is green and velvet-like. This lawn is a popular resort for many birds of the vicinity.

In England blackbirds, thrushes, robins, starlings, and sparrows are the birds which frequent lawns. Of these the sparrows are the only ones found in our Indian gardens. Sparrows are very partial to my lawn. Throughout the day numbers of them hop about on the turf, looking for objects so small that I have not been able to make out what they are. The fact that sparrows are greatly addicted to a lawn that is watered and mown twice a week serves to show that *Passer domesticus* is not so black as he is painted by his detractors. The sparrows cannot come to my lawn for any purpose other than that of looking for insects.

The first birds to visit the lawn every morning are a pair of coucals, or crow-pheasants (*Centropus sinensis*). They appear on the scene with great punctuality about an hour before sunrise. The crow-pheasant is one of the most familiar of Indian birds. It is neither a crow nor a pheasant, nevertheless there is much to be said in favour of its popular name, because the bird has altogether the appearance of a crow that has exchanged wings and tail with a pheasant. It is black all over save for its ruby-coloured eye and chestnut-hued wings. It belongs to the cuckoo family, but, unlike the majority of its brethren, builds a nest and incubates its eggs. It is characterised by an elongated hind toe, which he who lies behind the mosquito net may observe as its possessor struts by. There is something very pompous about the strut of the crow-pheasant. Were it an inhabitant of Whitechapel, its friends would undoubtedly enquire whether it was a fact that it had purchased the street! But the sight of an insect on the lawn causes the coucal to throw dignity to the winds. Its sedate walk becomes transformed into a bustling waddle as it gives chase to the insect with a gait like that of a stout, nervous lady hurrying across a road thronged with traffic. Crow-pheasants feed largely on insects, and it is in search of these that they frequent the lawn. Their food, however, is not confined to such small fry; they are very partial to snakes, and so are useful birds to have in the garden.

Hoopoes (*Upupa indica*) are constant visitors to my lawn. They revel in soft ground. The comparatively hard probe-like bill of the hoopoe enables the bird to extract insects from ground on which the soft-billed snipe could make no impression. But hoopoes prefer soft ground; from it they can obtain food with but little effort. Unfortunately for them, velvety lawns are not common in India; hence the birds flock to those that exist as eagerly as Europeans rush to the Himalayas in June. A few mornings ago I counted twenty-seven hoopoes feeding on my lawn. Occasionally a hoopoe perches on one of the bars from which my mosquito curtains hang, and thus unconsciously exposes himself to close scrutiny on my part. There are few birds so delightful to watch as hoopoes. Their form is unique. Their colouring is striking and pleasing. Then they are such fussy little creatures. When feeding they behave as if they were in a violent hurry. The *modus operandi* is a hasty tap of the bill here and another there, and if these reveal nothing promising, a few hurried steps, then more probing. The majority of these tappings and probings reveal nothing, but every now and then a spot is discovered beneath which an ant-lion, earthworm, or other creature lies buried. Then the fun waxes fast and furious; the hoopoe begins to excavate in real earnest, and plies its bill as eagerly as a terrier scratches away the loose earth that conceals its retreating quarry. After a few seconds this strenuous probing and digging usually results in some creature being dragged out of the earth. This is swallowed by the hoopoe after a little manipulation rendered necessary by the length of the bird's bill. Having disposed of its quarry the insatiable hoopoe passes on, without a pause, to seek for further victims. With twenty or thirty hoopoes thus at work, day after day, it is strange that the insect store of my lawn does not become exhausted.

While the hoopoe is feeding, its fan-like crest remains tightly closed. This attitude of the crest denotes business. The corona of the hoopoe is as mobile as are the ears of a horse. There is more expression in it than in the face of many a man or woman.

Mynas are, of course, always to be found on the lawn, but as these birds feed largely on grasshoppers, they seek their food by preference amid grass which is drier and longer than that of my lawn.

At the time when the grass is irrigated numbers

of pied mynas (*Sturnopastor contra*) and paddy-birds (*Ardeola grayii*) visit the lawn. The former strut about, and the latter stand near the place where the water trickles from the pipe. Both come in quest of creatures driven from their underground homes by the water.

Occasionally two or three crows visit the lawn; these come to gratify their curiosity rather than for food. Crows are inquisitive creatures, and cannot resist visiting any spot where they see other birds enjoying themselves. Wagtails are birds which are very partial to lawns, but all the Indian species, with one exception, leave India in April or May, so that their graceful forms do not delight the eye in the hot weather.

XV

THE GREY HORNBILL

HORNBILLS, like the Jews, are a peculiar race. There are no other birds like unto them. They are fowls of extravagant form. Their bodies are studies in disproportion. The beak and tail of each species would fit admirably a bird twice as big as their actual possessor, while birds less than half their size might well look askance at the wings with which hornbills are blessed. With the solitary exception of the "cake walk" of the adjutant (*Leptoptilus dubius*), I know of no sight in Nature more absurd than the flight of the hornbill. By dint of a series of vigorous flaps of its disproportionately short wings the bird manages to propel itself through the air. But the efforts put forth are too strenuous to be maintained for many seconds at a time. When it has managed to acquire a little impetus, the great bird gives its pinions a rest, and sails at a snail's pace for a few seconds, after which, in order to save itself from falling, it violently flaps its wings again, and thus manages to win its way laboriously from one grove to another, in much the same way as the primitive flying reptiles must have done. Nor is the excitement over when it reaches its destination. Owing to the weight of the beak, the hornbill is in danger of toppling over, head foremost, as it alights on a branch, and assuredly would sometimes do so but for the long tail which serves to balance the great beak. So vigorously does the hornbill have to flap its wings during flight that the sound of the air rushing through them can be heard for nearly half a mile in the case of the largest species.

All hornbills are grotesque. The grey species is, however, the least grotesque, and approaches the most nearly to the appearance of normal birds. Three species of grey hornbill occur in India. The common grey hornbill (*Lophoceros birostris*) is characterised by the possession of what is known as a casque—an appendage which the other two species of grey hornbill lack. This is a horny excrescence from the upper surface of the beak. In some species the casque is so large as to extend over the greater part of the head and beak. No one has yet discovered its use. I am inclined to think that it has no use. The Malabar and Ceylonese grey hornbills, whose habits are identical with those of the common grey hornbill, thrive very well, in spite of the fact that they have no casque.

Lophoceros birostris is a bird nearly two feet in length. The prevailing hue of the plumage is greyish brown. The bill, which is four inches long, and the casque are blackish. Like the other members of this peculiar family, the grey hornbill possesses eyelashes, which increase the strangeness of its appearance. This species is found in most parts of the plains of India, except the Malabar coast, where it is replaced by *Lophoceros griseus*. The grey hornbill of Ceylon is the species *L. gingalensis*.

The majority of species of hornbill shun the vicinity of human beings. They are accordingly to be found only in the Terai and other great forest tracts. The grey hornbill, on the contrary, shows no fear of man. Although strictly arboreal in its habits, it occurs in those parts of the country that are not thickly wooded. A grove of trees is all that it demands. Grey hornbills are birds of the highway and the village. Usually they go about in small flocks.

Lophoceros birostris is particularly abundant in the sub-Himalayan districts of the United Provinces. In Oudh and the eastern part of Agra almost every village has its colony of grey hornbills. These hamlets are nearly always surrounded by trees, usually bamboos, among which the hornbills live. In many parts of Northern India grey hornbills are commonly seen in the avenues of trees which are planted along the high roads to shelter wayfarers from the midday sun.

Hornbills feed largely on fruit and are fond of that of the pipal and the banian trees. Their great bills are admirably suited to the plucking of fruit. When the hornbill has severed a berry, it tosses it into the air, catches it in the bill as it falls, and then swallows it. This is the most expeditious way of passing the food from the tip of its bill to the entrance to its gullet.

The cry of the grey hornbill is feeble for so large a bird, and is querulous, like that of the common kite.

The nesting habits of the hornbills are very remarkable. The eggs are deposited in a cavity in a tree. The cavity selected may be the result of decay in the wood, or it may have been hollowed out by a woodpecker or other bird. In either case the hornbill has usually to enlarge the cavity, for, being a big bird, it requires a spacious nest. When all preparations have been made, the female enters the nest hole, and does not emerge until some weeks later, when the eggs have been hatched and the young are ready to fly. Having entered the nest, the hen hornbill proceeds to reduce the size of the orifice by which she gained access to the nest cavity, by plastering it up with her ordure until the aperture is no more than a mere slit, only just large enough to enable her to insert her beak through it. Thus, during the whole period of incubation and brooding she is entirely dependent on the cock for food. And he never leaves her in the lurch. He is most assiduous in his attentions. When he reaches the trunk in which his wife is sitting, he, while clinging to the bark with his claws, taps the trunk with his bill, and thus apprises her of his arrival. She then thrusts her bill through the orifice and receives the food. When at length the young are ready to leave the nest, the mother emerges with her plumage in a much-bedraggled condition.

Why the hen hornbill behaves thus, why she is content to submit periodically to a term of "simple imprisonment," is one of the unsolved riddles of

Nature. This curious habit is peculiar to the hornbills, but seems to be common to every member of the family. In this connection it is interesting to note that the hoopoes, which are nearly related to the hornbills, have somewhat similar nesting habits. The hen hoopoe, although she does not adopt the heroic measure of closing up the entrance to the nest cavity, is said never to leave the nest until the young have emerged from the eggs. No sight is commoner in India than that of a hoopoe carrying food to the aperture of a hole in a tree, or in a building made of mud, in which his spouse is sitting. Another curious feature in the nesting habits of the hornbill does not appear to have been mentioned by any observer, and that is that during the nesting season hornbills go about in threes, and not in pairs. I have noticed this on two occasions, and Mr. Horne, in his interesting account of the nesting of the grey hornbill at Mainpuri, which is recorded in Hume's *Nests and Eggs of Indian Birds*, mentions the presence of a third hornbill, who " used to hover about, watch proceedings, and sometimes quarrel with her accepted lord, but he never brought food to the female." Although grey hornbills are by no means uncommon birds, very few nests seem to have been taken. The result is that there are several points regarding their nidification that need elucidation. Those who love the fowls of the air should lose no opportunity of studying the ways of these truly remarkable birds.

XVI

THE FLAMINGO

ORNITHOLOGISTS, as is their wont, have disputed much among themselves as to whether the flamingo is a stork-like duck or a duck-like stork. Indians accept the former view and call the bird the King Goose (*Raj Hans*); their opinion was shared by Jerdon, who classed the flamingo among the geese. Likewise, Stuart Baker has given flamingos a place among the Indian ducks and their allies.

The flamingo is both wader and swimmer. It has long legs, the better to wade with, and webbed feet admirably adapted to natation. The bird certainly wades by preference. I have never seen it in water sufficiently deep to render swimming necessary or even possible. Those who have been more fortunate state that the swimming movements of the flamingo resemble those of a swan. I doubt whether flamingos ever swim from choice, but the webbed feet are likely to be useful, especially in the case of young birds, when flamingos are swept off their feet by the wind in a violent storm.

Two species of flamingo occur in India. These are

known as *Phœnicopterus roseus* and *P. minor*, or the common and the lesser flamingo. As the former is the one most often seen in India let us concentrate our attention on it. It is as tall as many a man, and measures over four feet from the tip of the beak to the end of the tail. Of these four feet the greater portion consists of neck, which is very supple; a flamingo when preening its feathers often twists the neck so that it assumes the shape of a figure of eight. The general hue of the bird is white tipped with rosy pink; the wings are crimson and black, hence the appropriate scientific name, *Phœnicopterus*, wings of flame. The bill is pale pink, tipped with black, while the legs are reddish pink.

Every Anglo-Indian has seen flamingos in the wild state, if not in India, at any rate from the deck of a ship as it crept through the Suez Canal. The shallow lakes and lagoons in the vicinity of the Canal abound with flamingos. These beautiful birds are to be seen in numbers throughout the cold weather in the shallow lakes and backwaters round about Madras. Flamingos are very numerous in Ceylon, where they are known to the Singalese as the "English Soldier Birds" on account of their "crimson tunics" and upright martial bearing.

A flock of flamingos is a fine spectacle. Some years ago I saw near the Pulicat Lake about two hundred of these birds. They were perhaps half a mile from the house-boat. Their white bodies showed up well against a background of blue water. Some of them were feeding with heads underwater, others stood as erect as soldiers at attention and as motionless as statues; a few were moving with great precision, like recruits under training. Portions of the flock were congregated in small groups, apparently in solemn conclave. Dignity and solemnity are the distinguishing features of the flamingo. After watching the flock for fully half an hour I fired a gun. I did not try to kill any of them. They were out of range. I fired because I wanted to see the birds take to their wings, to see them rise like a "glorious exhalation." The report of the gun seemed to cause no alarm. There was none of that fluster and hurry that most birds display when they hear the sound of firing. The flamingos rose in a stately manner; they did not all leave the water simultaneously. The birds took to their wings by twos and threes, so that it was not until more than a minute after the firing of the gun that all of them were in the air. As their wings opened the colour of the birds changed from white to crimson, the latter being the hue of the lining of their wings. It was as if red limelight had been thrown on to the whole flock.

During flight, the long white neck, that terminates in the pink-and-black bill, is stretched out in front, and the pink legs point behind, so that the neck and legs form one straight line, broken by the crimson wings, which are flapped very slowly. The great birds sailed thus majestically for a few hundred yards and then sank to the water.

When flamingos are about to alight the legs leave the horizontal position assumed during flight and come slowly forward until they touch the water. The whole flock settles without making any splash. It has never been my good fortune to watch the flight of flamingos at very close quarters. I will, therefore, reproduce from the *Saturday Review* Colonel Willoughby Verner's description of those he witnessed in Spain: "What a wonderful sight it was! The curious-shaped heads and bulbous beaks at the end of the long, thin, outstretched, and snake-like necks, the small compact bodies, shining white below and rosy pink above, the crimson coverts and glossy black of the quickly moving pinions, and the immensely long legs projecting stiffly behind, ending in the queer-shaped feet. Surely no other bird on God's earth presents such an incongruous and almost uncanny shape and yet affords such a beautiful spectacle of colour and movement. Onward they sped, now in one long sinuous line; now with some of the birds in the centre or rear increasing their speed and surging up 'line abreast' of those in front of them, and again falling back and resuming their posts, ever and anon uttering their weird, trumpeting, goose-like call. They were flying not fifteen feet above the water, and as they passed abreast of me, the moving mass of white, pink, crimson, and black was mirrored in the placid surface of the laguna below them which shone like a sheet of opal in the setting rays of the sun."

The beak of the flamingo is a curious structure. It is bent almost to a right angle in the middle, so that when the basal portion is horizontal the tip of the bill points towards the ground, and when the long neck is directed downwards (as must be done when the bird feeds because of the length of the legs) the terminal half of the bill is parallel to the ground, and the tip points between the bird's toes. Thus the flamingo when feeding assumes the position it would adopt when about to stand on its head! The upper mandible then is placed along the ground, and, for the convenience of the bird, is flattened, while the lower mandible, which is uppermost when the bird is feeding, is arched like the upper mandible in most birds. This arrangement gives the flamingo a grotesque appearance.

The food of this species consists of small crustaceans, insects and mollusca, together with vegetable matter. The quarry is scooped out of the mud at the bottom of the lake. The mandibles are lamellated like those of ducks, hence they, assisted by the tongue, act as sieves and reject most of the mud while retaining the nutritive material. The words "most of the mud" are used advisedly, for it is not possible to sift all out, so that those who have examined the contents of the stomach of the flamingo have usually found it to contain a quantity of sand and mud.

The nest of the flamingo is a mound of earth raised by the bird from shallow water. The only place in India where flamingos are known to breed is the Run of Cutch. In seasons when there has been sufficient rainfall this curious spot abounds with nests of flamingos.

The older writers believed that, on account of the length of its legs, the flamingo could not incubate its eggs in the ordinary manner. It was known that the nest consists of a mound raised from the ground, and from this it was conjectured that the bird stood up to hatch its eggs. Writing of the inconvenience of the long shanks of the flamingo, Bishop Stanley said:—

"A still greater inconvenience would ensue if it were under the necessity of sitting on its nest, like other birds, for it would then be utterly impossible to dispose of its long, stilted, disproportioned legs. Nature has, however, met the difficulty, and taught it how to make a nest exactly suited to its form and length of leg. It is made of mud, in the shape of a hillock, with a cavity on the top where the eggs are laid; and the height of the hillocks is such that she can sit as comfortably on her nest as a horseman does on his saddle, leaving her legs to hang dangling down at full length on either side."

In order to impress this peculiarity of the flamingo on the mind of the reader, the worthy Bishop furnishes a picture of an incubating flamingo. A similar belief used to exist regarding herons and other long-legged birds. These were supposed to sit astride the nest, and certain veracious observers stated that they had noticed the legs dangling down. Needless to state, there is no truth in these stories. Every long-shanked bird is able to bend its legs and tuck them up under it when necessary.

Mr. Abel Chapman has actually observed the flamingo folding its legs under its body when it is about to sit on the nest.

But it is unfair to laugh at good Bishop Stanley. His statement that the flamingo sits astride its nest is not nearly so ridiculous as Mr. A. Thayer's assertion that crocodiles mistake the flamingo for a sunset! Mr. Thayer is an American artist who is obsessed by the theory that, amid their natural surroundings, all birds and beasts are obliteratively coloured, so as to be completely invisible. Instead of meeting with the ridicule it deserves, this utterly preposterous theory appears to be accepted by some British zoologists!

Two eggs are usually laid by the flamingo, but only one seems to be hatched in the great majority of cases.

Baby flamingos are covered with greyish down, and have normally shaped bills, which, however, at an early age assume the curious form so characteristic of the adult.

XVII

SUMMER VISITORS TO THE PUNJAB PLAINS

DURING the months that Father Sol is doing his best to make the Punjab an earthly Inferno the birds are busy at their nests. They do not seem to mind the heat. Some of them positively revel in it, visiting us only in the hot weather. These summer visitors form an interesting group.

The bee-eaters are the first to make their appearance. In the first or second week in March, two species of bee-eater visit the Punjab—the little green one (*Merops viridis*), and the blue-tailed species (*M. philippinus*). The former is a grass-green bird about the size of a bulbul. Its beak is slightly curved and black; a bar of the same hue runs through the eye. The throat is a beautiful turquoise blue. The wings are tinted with bronze, so that the bird, when it flies, looks golden rather than green. The most distinctive feature of the bee-eater is the middle pair of tail feathers, which are blackish and project beyond the others as sharp bristles.

Bee-eaters feed upon insects which they catch on the wing. The larger species live up to their name by devouring bees and wasps. Like every other bird that hawks flying insects the bee-eater takes up a strategic position on a telegraph wire, a railing, a bare branch or other point of vantage, whence it keeps a sharp look-out for its quarry. When an insect appears it is smartly captured in the air, the mandibles of the bee-eater closing upon it with a snap, audible at a distance of several yards.

Bee-eaters begin nesting almost immediately upon arrival. The nest is a chamber, rather larger than a cricket ball, which the cock and hen, working turn about, scoop out of a sandbank with beak and claw. The nest chamber communicates with the exterior by a passage about three feet long, so narrow that the bird is unable to turn round in it. Every kind of sandbank is utilised. Numbers of nests are to be found in the mounds that adorn the Lawrence Gardens at Lahore. Others may be seen in the artificial bunkers on the uninviting *maidan* which is by courtesy called The Lahore Golf Links. The butts on the rifle range are sometimes made use of, the bee-eaters being utterly regardless of the bullets that every now and then bury themselves with a thud in the earth near the nest hole.

The blue-tailed bee-eater is distinguishable by its larger size, its yellowish throat, and its blue tail. It is not so abundant as the green species, and excavates its nest at a higher level. The note of both kinds of bee-eater is a soft but cheery whistle.

The honey-suckers (*Arachnechthra asiatica*) or sun-birds, as they are frequently called, follow hard upon the bee-eaters. As these charming little birds form the subject of a subsequent chapter, it is only necessary to state in this place that they build thousands of nests in the various stations of the Punjab during the summer months. At least, one nest is to be found in every garden. In each little nursery two or three families are reared in succession.

The koel (*Eudynamis honorata*) is perhaps the most interesting of our summer visitors. We are all of us acquainted with his fluty crescendo *ku-il, ku-il, ku-il,* also with the excited *kuk, koo-oo, koo-ooo,* which the bird pours forth in a veritable torrent.

The koel is sometimes erroneously called the brain-fever bird. This proud title properly belongs to another parasite, namely the hawk cuckoo (*Hierococcyx varius*), which does not come as far west as Lahore, but may be heard at Umballa. This noisy fowl shrieks *brain fever, brain fever, brain fever,* beginning low down in the scale and ascending higher and higher until his top note is reached, then he begins all over again, and repeats the performance for an indefinite period. He would have a future before him as a foghorn were it only possible to make him call at will!

The cock koel is a jet black bird with a red eye and a green bill. When flying he looks like a slenderly built, long-tailed crow. The hen is speckled black and white. This cuckoo cuckolds crows.

The cock draws off the owners of the nest by placing himself near them and screaming. The crows, being short-tempered birds, rise to the bait and give chase. While they are absent the hen slips into the nest and lays her egg. If sufficient time be allowed she destroys one or more of the eggs already in the nest.

She works hurriedly, for the operation is a dangerous one. If she be caught on the nest the crows will try to kill her and will, as likely as not, succeed. The life of the koel is by no means all beer and skittles. If the hen koel gets away before the crows return they fail to notice the strange egg, although it differs markedly from their blue and yellow ones, being smaller and olive green blotched with yellow. Nor do they seem to miss their own eggs which are lying broken on the ground beneath the nest. Sometimes the koel returns and lays a second egg in the same nest, and destroys all the legitimate eggs, for she can tell the difference between her eggs and those of the crow. Thus it sometimes happens that the deluded crows rear up only two koels. They never seem to notice the trick that has been played upon them. Even when the black-skinned young koels hatch out, the crows are apparently unable to distinguish them from their own pink-coloured young.

The young koel invariably emerges from the egg before his foster-brothers and thus begins life with a start. He develops much more quickly than they do, but, unlike the common cuckoo, ejects neither the other eggs in the nest, nor the young birds as they hatch out. He lives on good terms with the other occupants of the nest, and when fledged, makes laudable if ludicrous attempts to caw.

The natives assert that the hen koel keeps an eye on her offspring all the while they are in the crow's nest and takes charge of them after they leave it. I am almost certain that this is not so.

Early in April the paradise flycatchers (*Terpsiphone paradisi*) arrive. The hen is a chestnut bird with a black head and crest and a white breast; she looks something like a bulbul. The cock when quite young is similarly attired. At his first autumnal moult, that is to say when he is about fifteen months old, his two middle tail feathers outgrow the rest by twelve or thirteen inches. In his third year white feathers begin to appear among the chestnut ones, and after his third autumnal moult he emerges as a magnificent white bird with a metallic black head and crest. His elongated tail feathers now look like white satin streamers. He retains this livery for the remainder of his life, and looks so magnificent in it as to merit well his name. It is impossible to mistake the paradise flycatcher. There is no other bird like it. It is a denizen of orchards and shady groves and may always be seen during the hot weather in the beautiful wood on the bank of the Ravi between the bridge of boats and the railway. A cock paradise flycatcher, in the full glory of his white plumage, as he flits like a sprite through the leafy glade, is a sight never to be forgotten. The movements of his long tail feathers as he pursues his course are as graceful as those of the folds of the gossamer garments of a skilled serpentine dancer.

The nest is a deep cup, in shape like an inverted cone, plastered exteriorly with cobweb and white cocoons. It is almost invariably placed in a fork near the end of one of the lower branches of a tree. Both cock and hen take part in nest building and incubation. As the cock sits his long white tail feathers hang down over the side of the nest and render him very conspicuous. The most expeditious way of finding a paradise flycatcher's nest is to look out for a sitting cock. The alarm note of this species is a sharp harsh *Tschit*, but the cock is also able to warble a very sweet song.

The Indian oriole (*Oriolus kundoo*) is another gorgeous summer visitor to the Punjab. The cock is arrayed in rich golden yellow. His bill is pink and he has a black patch on each side of his head, there is also some black in his wings and tail. The hen is clad in greenish yellow and is neither so showy nor so handsome. The oriole is commonly called the mango bird by Europeans in India. I have never been able to discover whether the bird is so named because the cock is not unlike a ripe mango in colour, or because orioles are to be found in almost every mango tope. *Oriolus kundoo* is a bird of many notes. Of these the most pleasing is a mellow *lorio, lorio*. Another note very frequently heard is a loud but not unmusical *tew*. The alarm note of the species is a plaintive cry, not easy to describe. It is uttered whenever a human being approaches the nest. The hen alone incubates, but she is not often seen upon the nest, for she leaves it at the first sound of a human footfall.

The nest of the oriole is a wonderful structure. It is a cradle slung on to a stout forked branch. The bird tears with its beak strips of the soft bark from the mulberry tree. An end of the strip is wound round one limb of the fork, then the other end is passed under the nest and wound round the other limb of the supporting bough. If the strip be long enough it is again passed under the nest. This framework supports the nest proper, which is a hemispherical cup composed of fine roots and dried grass. The minimum of material is used in construction, with the result that the eggs lying in the nest are sometimes visible from below. He who would find orioles' nests should repair in June to the canal bank or to the above-mentioned wood.

Every oriole's nest that I have seen in Lahore has been placed near a king-crow's nest. It is, I think, for the sake of protection that the oriole builds near the king-crow. This latter is so pugnacious that most predaceous birds avoid the tree in which its nest is situated.

Among the summer visitors to the Punjab is a dove known as *Oenopopelia tranquebarica.* Those who find this name rather a mouthful are at liberty to call the bird the red turtle-dove. This species is of interest on account of the large amount of sexual dimorphism which it displays. The head and neck of the cock are ashy grey, his upper back and wings are the peculiar red of a faded port-wine stain, the lower back is grey, the middle tail feathers are brown and the other ones white. There is a black collar round his neck. The hen is a uniform greyish brown, her only adornment being a black collar similar to that of the cock.

As a chapter of this work is devoted exclusively to the red turtle-dove, nothing more need be said of it in this place, save that its note is not the orthodox coo, it is a peculiar low grunt, and gives one the impression that the bird has caught cold.

One summer visitor remains to be described, but he

need not detain us long, for, save his respectability, he has nothing in particular to commend him. I allude to the yellow-throated sparrow (*Gymnorhis flavicollis*). This bird probably sometimes passes for a hen house sparrow; close inspection, however, reveals a yellow patch on the throat. According to Jerdon this creature has much the same manners and habits as the common sparrow. This I consider libellous. The yellow-throated sparrow is a bird of retiring disposition and I have never heard of one forcing its way into a *sahib's* bungalow. It nestles in a hole in a tree. Having lined the ready-made cavity with dry grass and feathers, it lays four eggs which are thickly blotched all over with sepia, chocolate brown, or purple. A pair of these birds lives in the octagonal aviary at the Lahore Zoo.

XVIII

A BIRD OF MANY ALIASES

THE paddy bird has as many aliases as a professional criminal of twenty years' standing. I do not refer to his scientific names. Of course he has a number of these. Every bird has. A person who desires violent exercise for the memory cannot do better than try to keep pace with the kaleidoscopic changes which Indian ornithological terminology undergoes. The paddy bird is now known as *Ardeola grayii*, but I do not guarantee that he will be so called next month. When I assert that the paddy bird is a creature of many aliases, I mean that he has a number of popular names. He is sometimes known as the pond heron, because no piece of water larger than a puddle is too small to serve as a fishing ground for him. His partiality to flooded rice fields has given rise to the name by which he most commonly goes. He is frequently dubbed the blind heron, especially by natives. The Tamils call him the blind idiot. Needless to say the bird is not blind, its confiding disposition is responsible for the adjective. It might be blind for all the notice it takes of surrounding objects as it stands at the water's edge, huddled up like a decrepit old man.

Before proceeding further, let me, for the benefit of those who are unacquainted with the avifauna of India, describe the bird. It is much smaller than the common heron, being about the size of a curlew. The head, neck, and the whole of the upper plumage are greenish brown, each feather having a darker shaft stripe. The under parts are white, as are the larger wing feathers, but these latter are so arranged as to be altogether invisible when the wings are closed, so that the bird, when it flies, seems suddenly to produce from nowhere a pair of beautiful white pinions and sail away on them. Before it has flown far it usually performs the vanishing trick. This, like most effective conjuring tricks, is very easy to perform when one knows how to do it. The bird merely folds its wings, then the dark coverts alone are visible. These are of the same hue as the damp sand or mud on which the paddy bird spends a considerable portion of the day. The dingy hues of the paddy bird are the outcome of its habits; it is a *shikari* that stalks its prey or lies in wait for it. If it were as showy as the cattle egret its intended victims would "see it coming" and mock at it. Hence the necessity for its workaday garb.

The paddy bird is a very sluggish creature; it comes of a lazy family. There is not a single member of the heron tribe that does sufficient work to disqualify it for membership of the most particular trade union.

Most herons, however, do stalk their prey, which is more than the paddy bird usually does. One may sometimes see him progressing through shallow water at the rate of six inches a minute; but more commonly he stands in shallow water as motionless as a stuffed bird, with his head almost buried in his shoulders, looking as though he were highly disgusted with things in general. As a matter of fact he is thoroughly enjoying himself. His ugly eye is fixed upon some luckless frog in the water. The moment this comes within striking distance the pond heron will shoot out his long neck, seize the frog and swallow it whole. One cannot but feel sorry for the frog as it finds itself being hustled down the heron's throat. It probably mistook the motionless creature for a rock and, even had it not made this mistake, it could not be expected to know that the bird had buried in its shoulders a patent telescopic neck. After the amphibian is safely lodged *in ventro*, the paddy bird resumes his strategic position at the water's edge and maintains it for hours.

One day when I have nothing else to do I mean to mark down a paddy bird in its roosting tree, follow it to its fishing ground and picnic there all day and watch its behaviour. I shall then write an essay entitled *A Leaf from the Diary of a Lazy Bird.*

I imagine that the daily entry will read somewhat as follows:—

8 a.m.—(One hour after sunrise) woke up.

8—8.30—Pruned my feathers.

8.30—Flew to my fishing ground.

8.32—Settled there for the day.

8.40—9—Caught a few water insects for breakfast.

9—10—Had a nap.

10.30—Caught a frog.

10.32—12—Had a nap.

12.15—Caught another frog.

12.17—2—Had a nap.

2.20—Caught a third frog.

2.22—Walked three yards.

2.24—4—Had a nap.

4.40—Caught a fourth frog.

5—6—Had a nap.

6.15—6.30—Caught and ate my supper.

6.30—Flew to roost.

6.35—40—Had a row with a neighbour who had taken my private roosting site.

7 p.m. onwards—Slept the sleep of the just.

The above is not a statement of actual fact. Like many scientific productions it is based on imagination and not observation. I have not yet devoted a whole day to the paddy bird. I have, however, spent an hour at a pond heron's dormitory and record in the next chapter what I saw there.

At the nesting season the paddy birds awake from their habitual lethargy. Towards the end of June they begin to make a collection of sticks and pile these together on a forked branch high up in some tree. When the pile has reached a magnitude sufficient to support four or five eggs the paddy bird flatters itself that it has built a fine nest and forthwith proceeds to stock it with eggs. This species usually nests in colonies, sometimes in company with night herons (*Nycticorax griseus*), and occasionally with crows.

Seen from below the nursery looks rather like an old crow's nest. The eggs are a beautiful pale green. They are most jealously watched by the parents; one or other always remaining on guard, and, every now and then, gurgling with delight.

The youngsters hatch out in a comparatively advanced condition. A baby pond heron about a week old is a most amusing object. It has a long, narrow, pinkish beak, quite unlike the broad triangle that does duty for a mouth in passerine birds. Its neck is disproportionately long, while its green legs are many sizes too big for it. Downy feathers are scattered irregularly over the body, and add to the absurdity of its appearance. The eye is bright yellow and gives its possessor a very knowing look.

Most birds when they have young work like slaves to procure sufficient food for them. Not so the paddy bird. He knows a trick worth two of that. He is a past master in the art of loafing. He does not feed his offspring on tiny insects, dozens of which are required to make a decent meal; he forces whole frogs down the elastic gullet of the nestling. Now the most ravenous and greedy young bird cannot negotiate very many frogs per diem; hence the feeding of their young is not a great tax upon paddy birds.

XIX

PADDY BIRDS AT BEDTIME

THE paddy bird (*Ardeola grayii*) is at all times and all seasons as solemn as the proverbial judge; hence at bedtime, when all other birds are hilarious and excited, he is comparatively sedate.

Paddy birds, in common with the great majority of the feathered kind, roost in company. At sunrise, the company separates. Each goes his own way to his favourite river, paddy-field, tank, pond or puddle, as the case may be, and spends the day in morose solitude. At sunset he rejoins his fellow pond herons.

Growing out of the water in a small tank near the railway station at Fyzabad are three trees, one of which is quite small, while the other two are about the size of well-grown apple trees. This description is perhaps as vague as saying of an object that it is as big as a piece of chalk. I am sorry. I cannot help it. I know of no accurate method of judging the size of a tree that is surrounded by dirty, slimy water. On one of these trees, like unto an apple tree, over fifty paddy birds spend the night.

One might have thought that this was a very fair load for an average tree. This, however, is not the opinion of the feathered folk. Some 300 or 400 mynas also utilise this tree as a dormitory. The mynas occupy the higher branches, and the paddy birds the lower ones.

As every one knows, the roosting place of a company of mynas is a perfect pandemonium. For thirty or forty minutes before going to sleep each individual bird shouts at every other individual with truly splendid energy. If man could but devise some means of harnessing this energy, every station in India might be lighted with electric light at a very small cost. As things are, all this energy is dissipated in the form of sound, with the result that the noise made by 300 starlings can be heard at a distance of half a mile.

One might reasonably suppose that a quiet, sedate bird like *Ardeola grayii* would be greatly disgusted at the din that emanates from the throats of mynas at bedtime, and would refrain from selecting as his dormitory a tree that literally quivers with the shoutings of mynas. It is, however, not so. Birds rarely do what one would expect. I know hundreds of ideal sites for birds' nests that are never utilised. *Per contra*, I have met with numbers of nests situated in the most uncomfortable and evil-smelling places. Paddy birds obviously do not suffer from nerves.

For about fifteen minutes before and fifteen minutes after sunset the tree in which all these birds roost presents an animated appearance. One or two paddy birds are the first to arrive, and they settle on one or other of the lower branches which almost touch the water. Nearly all birds, on approaching the tree in which they roost, literally throw themselves into the foliage, they plunge into it at headlong speed. Needless to say, the paddy bird does nothing so reckless as this; nevertheless, when approaching the tree in which he intends to spend the night he travels faster than at any other time, except, of course, when he is being chased by a falcon. The advance-guard of the mynas arrives very shortly after the first *bagla.* The mynas belong to two species—the common and the bank mynas (*Acridotheres tristis* and *A. ginginianus*). They come in squads of twenty or thirty. The various squads arrive in rapid succession. Then the uproar begins and continues to swell in volume as the numbers in the tree increase.

The paddy birds come in ones and twos, and, as stated, invariably alight on one of the lower branches. They usually select a branch so thin that it would be impossible for so large a bird to obtain a foothold on it did not the claws of that bird grip like a vice; and even so it is not without much flapping of their white wings that the pond herons manage to reach a state of equilibrium.

If, when a paddy bird has succeeded in steadying itself on a slender branch two feet or so above the level of the water, another feckless fellow elects to alight on the selfsame branch, there follows trouble compared to which the Turco-Italian War is, as the babu says, a mere storm in a teapot; both birds seem in danger of taking a bath. On such occasions, the bird first on the tree greets the new-comer with gurgles of protest, there is much flapping of white wings, and eventually one or both the birds have to leave the branch.

But it is not until the tree is filled with birds that the real fun begins. When about forty paddy birds are squatting on the lower branches and over 300 mynas on the upper ones, it will be well understood that there is not much accommodation available for new arrivals. When a belated myna appears on the scene and plunges into the midst of his brother starlings, he is greeted with such a torrent of abuse that, although, in the gathering gloom, one cannot see what is going on amid the foliage, one feels convinced that the abuse is backed up by assault and battery. If, on the other hand, the luckless myna pitches into the tree at a lower elevation, he is liable to find himself transfixed by the stiletto-like beak of the nearest paddy bird, the savage thrust being accompanied by a lugubrious croak which seems to be the only note of the paddy bird. Nine out of ten mynas prefer incurring the wrath of their own kind to bringing down upon themselves the less noisy but more formidable anger of the pond heron.

If the mynas are packed like sardines in a box, the paddy birds lower down are not much more comfortable. It is true that the paddy birds are not squeezed together after the manner of the mynas, for the simple reason that if more than two of them attempted to squat on any but the stoutest of the branches they would all find themselves immersed in the slimy, unsavoury water beneath. The discomfort of the paddy birds is of another kind. Each one is balancing himself on an insecure perch and lives in momentary terror of being displaced by the advent of some other *bagla*. Hence, when the tree contains about forty herons, every fresh arrival is greeted with croaks the most sepulchral, and there is much shaking of branches and flapping of wings before he can find a spot on which he is able to maintain himself in a state of unstable equilibrium.

I watched the tree in question one evening in order to ascertain how many paddy birds roosted in it. I was able to count fifty-four by enumerating the birds as they arrived. I may have missed a few. But this is a mere detail. The lower branches carried all the paddy birds they were capable of bearing with safety. A few of the paddy birds had to be content with berths in a neighbouring tree, which grew out of the water at a distance of a few feet.

Some time after the sun had set one of the overflow party decided to try his luck in the main tree, and this resulted in such croaking and fluttering of wings on the part of his fellow paddy birds that for a few seconds the din of the mynas was drowned.

By the time it is really dark every bird, be he myna or pond heron, is sufficiently satisfied to hold his tongue. From then until an hour before sunrise not a sound emanates from the sleeping population of some 400 mynas and 50 paddy birds, who have elected to spend the night amid the unwholesome vapours that emanate from the water below. Birds are evidently mosquito proof.

XX

MERLINS

MERLINS are pigmy falcons. Like falcons, they are reclaimed for hawking purposes, but are regarded as mere toys by those who indulge in " the sport of kings."

In the days when falconry was a fashionable pastime in England nearly every lady of quality possessed a merlin, which was often as much of a companion as a dog is nowadays. The exquisite little bird of prey would accompany its mistress on her rides or her walks, flying overhead and coming to the glove when called. This species, being the only kind of merlin found in England, is popularly called the merlin (*Æsalon regulus*), even as *Cuculus canorus* is always known as the cuckoo, as though it were the only cuckoo in the world.

The merlin when trained for falconry is usually flown at the skylark. There are few prettier sights than that presented by a contest between a merlin and a skylark. Both know that the merlin can do nothing until it gets above its quarry; hence the contest at first resolves itself into one for supremacy of position. The adversaries often fly upwards in spirals until they almost disappear from view. When once the merlin does succeed in getting above the lark it makes swoop after swoop until it strikes its quarry.

In India the merlin is often trained to fly at the hoopoe. This contest is of a nature very different from that just described. The hoopoe does not rely on speed. It trusts to its truly marvellous power of timing the onslaught of the merlin and swerving at the critical moment, so that the merlin misses it by a hair's breadth. So great a master of aerial manœuvre is the hoopoe that two merlins working together are required to accomplish its downfall.

As the plumage of *Æsalon regulus* has the nondescript colouring that characterises most birds of prey, no useful purpose will be served by an attempt to describe it. The merlin is a winter visitor to India, and visits only the Punjab and Sind.

There is, however, another species of merlin which is a permanent resident in and distributed throughout India, viz. the red-headed merlin (*Æsalon chicquera*) or turumti as the bird is popularly called. Like the common merlin it is one of the smaller pirates of the air, being no larger than a myna, but it is the very quintessence of ferocity, and it knows not what fear is. Hence it is a terror to many creatures of greater magnitude than itself. The red-headed merlin is comparatively easy to identify, because it has some distinctive colouring, in the shape of a chestnut-red head and neck. The remainder of the upper plumage is French grey, marked with fine brown cross-bars. There is a broad black band with a white edge across the end of the tail. The chin, throat, and under parts are white, with brown spots, which become less plentiful as the individual grows older. This disappearance with age of the markings on the lower parts is very common among birds of prey, and is one of the many problems of animal colouring that do not appear to be explained by the theory of natural selection.

The hen turumti is about fourteen inches in length, of which six consist of tail. The cock, as is usual among raptores, is somewhat smaller than the hen.

The red-headed merlin occurs only in India. It is an evil manufactured for the sole benefit of the small birds of Hindustan. The turumti does not appear to undergo any periodical migration. It preys chiefly upon small birds. Social larks, little ringed plovers and sparrows are its commonest victims. But it is not afraid to tackle larger birds. Frequently it attacks mynas, starlings, quails, and doves. Indeed the usual lure bird for a red-headed merlin is a myna. This is tethered to a stick stuck into the ground, and in front of it is stretched a net attached to upright posts. The first turumti to observe this swoops down at the myna to find itself hopelessly entangled in the net. Hume once saw a red-headed merlin strike a pigeon and kill it with the first blow. Turumtis do not confine their attention to birds. The alert little palm squirrel is often victimised, as are sometimes those bats that are so unwary as to venture forth before the merlins go to bed.

When pursuing their operations in the open turumtis frequently hunt in couples, and, as they fly exceedingly swiftly, no matter how speedy the quarry be or how adept in swerving in the air, it is rarely able to escape from the concerted attack of a pair of these little furies.

Red-headed merlins are addicted to perching on the telegraph wires that are stretched alongside railway lines. They do this in order to pounce down into the midst of a flock of small birds alarmed by the noise of a passing train. The turumti, like the sparrow hawk, is a sprinter rather than a long-distance flier, and hence is able to secure its quarry in gardens, groves, and other comparatively confined places. It is fond of gliding with great rapidity along some hedgerow or bank and swooping down on any small bird feeding in the vicinity.

The turumti is not often used for purposes of falconry, which is somewhat surprising, seeing that it affords better sport than does the shikra, because it does not give up the chase so readily. When trained it is usually flown at the blue jay or roller (*Coracias indica*). "In pursuit of this quarry," writes Jerdon, "the falcon follows most closely and perseveringly, but is often baulked by the extraordinary evolutions of the roller, who now darts off obliquely, then tumbles down perpendicularly, screaming all the time and endeavouring to gain the shelter of the nearest grove or tree. But even here he is not safe; the falcon follows him from branch to branch, and sooner or later the exhausted quarry falls a victim to the ruthless bird of prey."

Very different is the behaviour of the shikra; he makes a dash at the quarry, and, if he fail to seize it at once, gives up the chase.

The red-headed merlin is thrown from the hand in the same way as the shikra. According to Mr. R. Thompson, the turumti affords peculiar sport with the spotted dove (*Turtur suratensis*), "striking at the quarry several times, and even often losing it altogether, owing partly to the softness of the dove's feathers, which give way at the least touch, and partly to its rapid dodging flight."

Turumtis breed from February to June, earlier in South India than in the Punjab and the Himalayas. The nest is usually built in a fork near the top of a tree—a tamarind or a mango for preference. In size and appearance the nest resembles that of a crow. It consists of a conglomeration of twigs, forming a platform of which the diameter measures about a foot. In the middle is a depression, lined with fine twigs, roots, feathers, or other convenient materials, in which the eggs are placed. Both sexes take part in nest building, which they appear to consider a very difficult and arduous task, judging by the fuss they make over the placing of every twig brought to the nest. The eggs are reddish white, very thickly speckled with brownish red. Turumtis are exceedingly pugnacious at the nesting season, and are as resentful as king-crows at any kind of intrusion; hence they are kept busy in giving chase to crows *et hoc genus omne*, who seem to take a positive delight in teasing fussy birds with nests.

XXI

THE COMMON WRYNECK

I LEAVE it to anatomists to determine whether wrynecks are woodpeckers that are turning into other birds, or other birds that are changing into woodpeckers. Certain it is that they are closely allied to woodpeckers.

Only four species of wryneck are known to exist, and, of these, three are confined to the Dark Continent, while the fourth is a great traveller. It is the bird which is frequently seen in India during the winter, and is well known in England as the "cuckoo's mate," because it migrates every year to Great Britain at the same time as the cuckoo. Ornithologists call this bird *Iynx torquilla*, plain Englishmen usually term it the wryneck, as though there were only one species in the world. From their insular point of view they are quite right because it is the only wryneck they ever see unless they leave their island. One convenience of living in a country, like England, poor in species, is that to particularise a bird is rarely necessary; it is sufficient to speak of the cuckoo, the swallow, the kingfisher, the heron. On the other hand, we who dwell in this country of many species, if we would not be misunderstood, usually have to particularise the cuckoo, the kingfisher, or the swallow of which we are speaking. However, as regards wrynecks, India is no better off than England. One species only visits that country; hence Indians may indulge in the luxury of speaking of it as the wryneck. This is a bird not much larger than a sparrow and attired as plainly as the hen of that species. But here the resemblance ends. The wryneck is as retiring in disposition as the sparrow is obtrusive. I defy any one to dwell a week in a locality that boasts of a pair of sparrows without noticing them, but many a man spends the greater part of his life in India without once observing a wryneck. The greyish-brown plumage of the wryneck, delicately mottled and barred all over with a darker shade of brown, harmonises very closely with the trunks of trees or the bare earth on which it spends so much of its time, and thus it often eludes observation.

The wryneck, like its cousins the woodpeckers, feeds almost exclusively on insects which it secures by means of the tongue. This wormlike structure is several inches in length and is hard and sharp, barbed at the tip and covered elsewhere with very sticky saliva. It can be shot out suddenly to transfix the bird's quarry, and then as rapidly retracted. The tongue is so long that when retracted it coils up inside the head. Although wrynecks feed a good deal on trees, they are far less addicted to them than woodpeckers are. The latter sometimes feed upon the ground, but this is the exception rather than the rule, while with the wryneck the reverse holds good. Once, at Lahore, I nearly trod upon a wryneck that was feeding on the ground. It flew from between my boots to a low bush hard by; then it descended to the ground and began to feed in the grass. I crept towards the place where it was feeding, and it did not again take to its wings until I was close up to it. This time it flew to a branch of a tree about ten feet above the level of the ground. I again followed up the wryneck. This time it allowed me to walk right up under it, and study the dark cross-bars on its tail feathers. After a little time it betook itself to a bunker on the golf links, from off which it began to pick insects. Then it flew to a low bush, and from thence dropped to the ground. I again followed it up, and, as I approached, it quietly walked away. Other naturalists have found the wryneck in India equally tame. Mr. Blyth says of it: "Instinctively trusting to the close resemblance of its tints to the situations on which it alights, it will lie close and sometimes even suffer itself to be taken by the hand; on such occasions it will twirl its neck in the most extraordinary manner, rolling the eyes, and erecting the feathers of the crown and throat, occasionally raising its tail and performing the most ludicrous movements; then, taking advantage of the surprise of the spectator, it will suddenly dart off like an arrow."

At most seasons of the year the wryneck is a remarkably silent bird. I do not remember ever having heard one utter a sound in India. When, however, it first arrives in England it has plenty to say for itself. "In one short season," says an anonymous writer in England, "we hear its singular monotonous notes at intervals through half the day. This ceases, and we think no more about it, as it continues perfectly mute; not a twit or a chirp escapes to remind us of its sojourn with us, except the maternal note or hush of danger, which is a faint, low, protracted hissing, as the female sits clinging by the side or on the stump of a tree."

The wryneck is not singular among birds in uttering its note only at certain seasons of the year. Very few of the song birds pour forth their melody all the year round. This fact bears powerful testimony to the view I have frequently enunciated as to the nature of birds' song. There is nothing conversational in it, nothing in the nature of language; it is merely the expression of superabundant vitality which fills most birds at certain seasons of the year.

Like very many other migrants, the wryneck does not appear to be powerful on the wing. Its flight has been well described as "precipitate and awkward."

The wryneck derives its name from a curious habit it has of twisting its neck as it seeks for insects on a tree-trunk or mound.

Wrynecks are very rarely seen in cages or aviaries, probably because they are not songsters and because their habits are not such as to render them attractive in an aviary. Nevertheless, wrynecks thrive in captivity. Bishop Stanley records an instance of a wryneck which "lived for a year and a half in a cage, and never appeared to show impatience during its confinement; it was observed always to take its food by throwing out its long tongue."

During the winter the wryneck seems to visit all parts of India, except possibly the Malabar coast, and it is sufficiently common in South India to have a Tamil name—*Moda nulingadu*.

The wryneck breeds neither in the plains of India nor, I believe, in the Himalayas, but its nest has been recorded in Kashmir. It busies itself with parental duties in the summer—in May and June in England—laying its glossy white eggs in a hollow in a tree. Unlike the woodpecker the wryneck does not hollow out its hole for itself. It is sensible enough not to undertake that which can be equally well done by others. In this respect, as in so many others, it differs from the woodpeckers proper.

XXII

GREEN PIGEONS

GREEN birds are comparatively few in number, but nearly all of those that do exist are very beautiful objects. Green is a colour which is rarely found alone in birds. The fowls of the air of which the plumage is mainly green almost invariably display patches of other colour. In the familiar green parrots red, pink, blue, and black occur; the green coppersmith flaunts the most gaudy hues of red, crimson, and yellow; the emerald merops adorns itself with gold and turquoise ornaments; while green pigeons are birds which display the whole spectrum of colours, each in a subdued form. In the common Indian species the forehead is greenish yellow; the nape and sides of the head French grey; the chin and neck are old gold shading off into olive; the body is greenish olive; the shoulder is washed with lilac. The primary wing feathers are dark grey, while the secondaries are similarly coloured, but have pale yellow tips. The tail is slate-coloured, becoming greenish yellow at the base. The feathers under the tail are a dark claret colour with creamy bars. The lower parts are slate-coloured tinged with green, save for the feathers of the thigh, which are canary yellow. The legs are orange yellow. The eye is blue, with an outer ring of carmine. Yet, notwithstanding all this show of colour, there is nothing gaudy about the green pigeon. Every tint is most delicately laid on, and each hue blends into the surrounding ones in a truly exquisite fashion, so that it is no exaggeration to call the green pigeon a vision of perfect loveliness.

In the unlikely event of any one taking the trouble to compare the above description with those given in the fauna of British India for *Crocopus phœnicopterus* (the Bengal green pigeon) and *C. chlorogaster* (the Southern green pigeon), that person will observe that it does not tally exactly with either of them. Nevertheless, my description is taken from a specimen shot by me in the Basti district of the United Provinces. The fact of the matter is that in places where the Bengal form meets the southern species the two interbreed, as, I believe, do all, or nearly all, allied species at the point of junction. And, in such cases, the hybrid birds appear to be perfectly fertile and to thrive equally with the parent species; neither of which would be the case were facts in accordance with the Wallaceian theory. But, as we shall see later, green pigeons seem to lay themselves out to destroy the biological orthodoxy of to-day.

Green pigeons appear to live exclusively on fruit. They go about in small flocks, seeking out trees of which the fruit is ripe; when they hit upon such a tree they behave as if they were schoolboys let loose in a tuck shop!

The Hindustani name for the green pigeon is *Harrial.* The natives, or at any rate some of them, assert that the bird never descends to the ground, because when its foot touches the earth the bird loses a pound in weight, in other words, shrivels up into nothingness! If asked how it drinks, they will reply that it settles on a reed which bends with its weight, so that it is able to partake of the water beneath without touching the earth. In the absence of a conveniently situated reed, the green pigeon overcomes the difficulty by carrying a twig in its feet. It would be interesting to discover the origin of this story, which is on a par with that which asserts that the red-wattled lapwing (*Sarcogrammus indicus*) sleeps on its back with its legs in the air, in order to be ready to catch the sky on its feet if ever this should fall! As a matter of fact green pigeons are very arboreal in their habits. I do not remember ever having seen one of them on the ground.

The note of the green pigeons is not a coo, but a pleasant whistle. The birds are sometimes caged on account of their song. But they are uninteresting pets. In captivity they soon lose their beauty, because they are so gluttonous as to smear the head and neck with whatever fruit be given them to eat.

Green pigeons are said to be far less obtrusive in their courtship than the majority of their kind. The male does hot puff himself out after the manner of other cock pigeons, but is content to bow before his lady love and in this attitude move his expanded tail up and down.

There are few birds that assimilate so closely to their surroundings as green pigeons. Fifty of them may be perched in a pipal tree, and a man on the look-out for them may fail to detect a single individual until one of the birds moves. They are thus excellent examples of protectively coloured birds. Their green livery undoubtedly affords them a certain amount of protection, and so may perhaps be considered a product of natural selection. Be this as it may, a consideration of the details of the colouring of their plumage shows that many of these, as, for example, the lilac on the wing, are quite unnecessary for the concealment of the bird. The eastern and the southern species which occur together in certain places and the hybrids produced by the interbreeding of these are all equally difficult to distinguish from the surrounding leaves, notwithstanding the fact that their plumage differs in details, e.g. the breast and the abdomen are greenish yellow in the southern and ashy-grey in the eastern form, while there is green in the forehead and tail of the latter, but not of the former. Thus we have two species of green pigeon, of which at least one has not originated by natural selection. Facts such as these, however, do not prevent Dr. Wallace, Sir E. Ray Lankester, and Professor Poulton continually proclaiming from the housetops that every existing species owes its origin to natural selection and nothing but natural selection!

There are several genera of green pigeons, and all of

them are characterised by short legs and broad toes. These are adaptations to the arboreal habit, in the formation of which natural selection has, in all probability, played an important part. The habits of all the genera are identical. They, one and all, build the rough-and-ready shakedowns which do duty for nests amongst the *Columbidæ*. All lay the inevitable two white eggs. Yet the sexes of the genus *Crocopus* are alike in external appearance, while those of the genera *Osmosteros*, *Sphenocercus*, and *Treron* exhibit considerable dimorphism. Again in the genus *Butreron* the sexual differences displayed are inconsiderable. These facts, of themselves, are quite sufficient to disprove the theory that sexual dimorphism in birds is due to the hen's greater need of protection. Cock green pigeons assimilate so well to their leafy environment that there cannot possibly be any necessity for their wives to be differently dressed. Further, it is worthy of note that the most flourishing of the genera of green pigeons is that in which the sexes dress alike.

XXIII

BULBULS' NESTS—I

IN May, 1911, a pair of red-whiskered bulbuls (*Otocompsa emeria*) took up their residence in my verandah at Fyzabad, that is to say, they spent the greater part of the day there in constructing a nest in a croton plant. The nest of the bulbul is a shallow cup, formed of bast, roots, twigs, and grass, loosely worked together. Sometimes dead leaves, pieces of rag and other oddments are woven into the fabric of the nest. The pair of bulbuls of which I write did not, however, indulge in any of these luxuries; they were content with a rudely constructed nursery. When the nest was nearly complete the owners deserted it. Why they acted thus I have not been able to discover.

The bulbuls absented themselves for a few days. When they returned they frequented another portion of the verandah, and their fussiness betrayed the fact that they were working at another nest. Several days passed before I found time to look for their nest, and I then discovered it in an aralia plant growing in the verandah, in a large pot placed at the right-hand side of one of the doors leading into my office room. The site chosen was the more remarkable in that it was within ten feet of the carpet on which the *chaprassis* sit when not engaged in active work. This nest was of even rougher design than the first one, and was equally devoid of decoration. So carelessly had it been constructed that, to use a nautical expression, it had a distinct list. I found in the nest three pinkish eggs, mottled and blotched with purplish red. They had been laid some time before I first saw them. This was demonstrated by the reluctance of the hen to leave the nest when I approached. Among birds the parental instinct increases as incubation proceeds. On one occasion the bird sitting on the nest in question allowed me to stroke its tail. This organ projects upwards like a semaphore, the nest not being sufficiently large to accommodate it.

It was not until the 15th July that I had leisure to watch these bulbuls closely. Up to that time I had merely noticed that both birds incubate, and that both sexes, and not the cock alone, as some writers assert, have the red "whiskers," or feathers, on the cheeks.

The weather being warm, it was not necessary for the birds to sit continuously, and the eggs were frequently left for ten minutes or longer at a time. On the morning of the 15th July, I found that two of the young birds had hatched out. Both parents were feeding them.

Birds are creatures of habit. Each parent bulbul had its own way of approaching the nest and of perching when tending the nestlings, so that, although I was not able to say for certain which of the pair was the cock and which the hen, I could distinguish one individual from the other. For brevity I will call them A and B, respectively.

Both birds, before flying to the nest, used to alight on the stem of a palm standing in the verandah. From this point their manœuvres differed. Individual A invariably flew to a stout vertical branch of the aralia, remained there for a second or two, flitted to a second vertical branch, and from thence hopped on to the edge of the nest, so that its face when there pointed to the east. This individual always showed itself the bolder spirit of the two. The other bird, B, used to fly from the palm to a slender leafy branch of the aralia, and thus cause considerable commotion among the leaves; from thence it jumped on to the edge of the nest, where it perched with its face pointing to the north. The *modus operandi* of A was the superior. The verandah faces the east, so that when A wished to leave the nest, it had but to jump across it into the space beyond, and then wing its way ahead, while B had to turn round before it could fly off. The neatness and address with which A used to leap across the nest into the air baffles description.

The 16th July fell on a Sunday. I therefore determined to devote some hours to studying the ways of those bulbuls at the nest. Every naturalist has his own method of prying into the ways of the fowls of the air or the beasts of the field. Some expose themselves to the Indian sun at midday in May, others will squat for hours in feverish swamps. People who do these things are worthy of all praise. I prefer less heroic methods. Accordingly, I had the pot containing the nest-bearing plant moved a distance of rather less than a yard, so that it stood in the middle of the doorway. I then had an easy chair placed in the office room at a distance of some four feet from the nest. Finally, I removed such of the leaves as tended to obstruct my view. Thus, I was able to watch the bulbuls through the *chik* in comfort, reclining in the easy chair.

Both parent birds were present when the plant was being moved. They looked rather alarmed, but raised no outcry. They did not seem eager to approach the nest after the position of the aralia had been changed. Evidently they did not understand the meaning of what they had seen. Eventually bulbul A summoned sufficient courage to visit the nest, and must have been highly gratified to find the two youngsters and the egg safe. While perching on the nest it kept its eye on me, having espied me, notwithstanding the fact that there was a *chik* between me and it. While eyeing me it cocked its head on one side and half opened its bill. The opening of the bill is an expression of anger. The bulbul's crest was also folded back, but this does not necessarily denote anger. The crest invariably assumes this attitude when the bulbul is incubating, or brooding, or feeding its young. It was some time before bulbul B could bring itself to visit the nest. It made at least six abortive attempts before it reached the edge of the nest, and then perched only for a second before flying off with every sign of trepidation. And for the whole of that day it showed itself nervous, whereas A soon came quite boldly to the nest. The difference in temperament between the two birds was most marked.

The parent birds did not come to the nest with the bill very full. They were usually content to bring one succulent grub or insect at a time.

In the earliest stages of their existence bulbul nestlings are so small that one caterpillar satisfies their hunger completely for some little time. So that it often happened that one of the parents arrived with food for which neither of the young birds was ready. Under such circumstances, the parent, after trying to force the food into the mouth of each nestling, remained on the rim of the nest waiting patiently until one of the youngsters lifted up its head for food. The baby bulbuls did not display at this early stage of their existence that eagerness for food, amounting almost to greediness, that characterises nestlings when they grow a little older.

On arrival with food the adult bird invariably uttered a couple of tinkling notes as if to inform its offspring that it had brought food. No sound emanated from the young birds during the first two or three days of their existence. When it had disposed of the food it had brought, the parent bird usually looked after the sanitation of the nest by picking up and eating the excreta. The parent birds did not appear ever to bring water to the nestlings. The succulent food probably supplies the requisite moisture. About midday on the 16th July the third young bird hatched out. The egg was intact at 10 a.m., but by a few minutes after midday the youngster had emerged, and half the shell was still in the nest. Thus the latest arrival made his appearance at least twenty-eight hours after either of his brethren.

I watched carefully in order to ascertain how the parent birds got rid of the egg-shell. Presently bulbul A came to the nest with food. When it had disposed of this, it began pecking in the nest, and appeared to be eating up the shell, but in reality it was cleaning the nest. After being thus engaged for a couple of minutes it flew off, carrying the half egg-shell in its beak. It flew to a distance with this, so that I did not see what became of it. This explains why broken egg-shells are seldom found lying on the ground below a nest. On the following day I placed a small piece of paper in the nest. This was carried off by the first parent bird to visit the nest, but not before the bird had fed its young. Shortly afterwards I placed a sheet of thick paper over the top of the nest so as to completely cover it. This non-plussed both parents. They made no attempt to insert their heads underneath it, but hopped about near the nest looking very disconsolate. I therefore removed the obstruction.

Young bulbuls when first hatched out are almost lost in the nest, taking up very little more room than the eggs that contained them; but they grow at an astonishing rate. By the time the oldest was six days old the three young birds almost filled the nest. From the fourth day the heads of the nestlings went up, and the mandibles vibrated rapidly whenever a parent approached; previously the young birds did not seem to hear the approach of the old birds. On the sixth day of their existence the youngsters first began to call for food, and for a time the sounds they emitted were very feeble. On the sixth day their eyes began to open, the opening at first being a tiny slit.

The parents were not always judicious in selecting food for their babes. I saw a bulbul bring a large insect with gauzy wings to a six-day-old nestling. The bird succeeded in ramming about one-third of it into the gaping mouth of the young one. The latter then made frantic efforts to swallow its prize. After struggling for the greater part of a minute it rested for a few seconds with half an inch of insect projecting from its bill. When at last it did succeed in swallowing it, the young bulbul fell back with neck stretched out and appeared to be in a thoroughly exhausted condition.

A triple tragedy has now to be related. Tragedies, alas! are very common among the bulbul community. On several occasions have I watched the nesting operations of these birds, but never yet have I seen a single young one reach maturity. When the eldest of the nestlings was seven days old I noticed that the list on the nest had become very marked, and on examining the nursery I found it empty. I then saw two of the young bulbuls lying on the floor of the verandah. The third was nowhere to be seen. Having rectified the position of the nest, I replaced the two nestlings, which the parents continued to feed. They did not seem to notice that one of their babes was missing.

On the following morning I found the nest half torn from its holdings, and saw the two youngsters on the earth near the roots of the aralia. Some leaves were strewn on the ground. Apparently a cat, a mongoose, or other predaceous creature had attempted to capture the parent bird during the night when it was sitting on the nest. It had not succeeded in the attempt, for both the old birds were hale and hearty; nevertheless, the fall had killed one of the youngsters. I placed the nest higher up in the aralia, in what I considered a safer situation, wedging it tightly between some branches, and then replaced the remaining nestling. This the parents continued to feed, although they seemed to find the nest difficult of access in its new position. The next morning I found the young bird alive and well in the nest, but this latter was now a lower branch of the aralia, to which it had been tied by string. Some officious *chaprassi* had doubtless done this. He had probably found the nest pulled down as I had found it on the previous day. Our efforts, however, were of no avail. On the following morning I again found the nest torn down, and this time the young bird was lying lifeless on the ground. The parents were somewhat disconsolate, and hung about for a little with food in their bills. But they soon seemed to realise that it was useless to bring food to a little bird that would not open its mouth. So they went off. They are, I believe, looking out for a suitable nesting site at the opposite end of my verandah. Bulbuls are as philosophical as they are foolish.

BULBULS' NESTS—II

The simplest observations often bring to light the greatest scientific truths. The force of gravity was revealed to Sir Isaac Newton by the falling of an apple. A kettle of boiling water gave the idea of the steam-engine to James Watt. The watching of bulbuls, which are so common in our Indian gardens and verandahs, suffices, apart from all other evidence, to demonstrate how erroneous is the orthodox doctrine that the survival of the fittest is the result of a struggle for existence among adult organisms. This year (1912) six bulbul tragedies have occurred in my garden, and the year is yet young.

The scene of one of these tragedies was the identical plant in which occurred the disaster described above, which happened about nine months ago. Thus we see that among bulbuls destruction takes place mostly in the nest, whole broods being wiped out at a time. The same is, I believe, true to a large extent of other species that build open nests. There are three critical stages in the life of a bird—the time when it is defenceless in the egg, the period it spends helpless in the nest, and the two or three days that elapse after it leaves the nest until its powers of flight are fully developed. When once a little bird has survived these dangerous periods, when it has reached the adult stage, it is comparatively immune from death until old age steals upon it. If zoologists would perceive this obvious truth there would be an end to nine-tenths of the nonsense written about protective colouring. Most birds are not protectively coloured; moreover, if they were so clothed as to be invisible amid their natural surroundings they would not derive much profit therefrom.

The labour of the six-and-twenty little bulbuls who, to my knowledge, have failed to rear their broods has not been lost altogether, for it has taught me something about their ways that I did not know before. Those birds showed me how quickly they are able to build a nest.

Very few observations regarding the duration of nest-building operations are on record. The reason is not far to seek. A nest at the very beginning of its existence is difficult to discover, and if come upon by chance is not easy to recognise as an incipient nursery. The nests we find are usually complete or in an advanced stage of construction.

I was strolling in the garden about 8 a.m. on the 3rd March last, when I noticed a bulbul with a leaf in its bill. I saw the bird fly into a small cypress bush and then emerge therefrom without the leaf. A short search sufficed to reveal the place in the bush where the leaf had been deposited. Placed by this leaf I found another leaf, a small branch of Duranta with some yellow berries attached to it, two or three small straws and some cobweb. These apparently had been thrown haphazard into the bush. Had I not seen the bulbul go into the bush carrying a leaf, I should not have suspected that these few things were the beginning of a nest, for they had no semblance of one. The bulbuls could not have been working at that nest for more than half an hour when I discovered it. On my return thirty minutes later to look at it I found that the amount of material collected had doubled, but the nest was still without any definite form; it was a mere conglomeration of rubbish. The two leaves already mentioned had dropped down nearly a couple of inches below the other material. The additional material consisted of more Duranta twigs with berries, straws, dried grasses, cobweb, and a piece of what looked like tissue paper. Half an hour later the rapidly increasing collection included a long piece of worsted, but this was not wound round any of the branches. In most bulbuls' nests that I have seen a certain amount of cotton or such-like material is used to support the cup-like nest by being bound to one of the neighbouring branches, although cobweb is the chief means of attaching the nest to its surroundings. In this particular instance, however, the worsted was not so utilised; possibly the pliable, upright branches of the cypress did not lend themselves to this kind of attachment. At this time (9 a.m.) the collected materials had nothing of the shape of a nest, but some of the tiny twigs were entwined in the cypress branches.

At midday, four hours after I had first seen the nest, I was astonished to find that it had assumed a saucer-like form. I was not a witness of the process whereby the original shapeless mass was made to take this shape, but my observations on other nests have convinced me that the nest is shaped entirely by the bird's body and feet. When a bulbul brings material to the nest, it drops this on to what has already been collected, sits on it, and proceeds to arrange it with its feet, which work so vigorously as to shake the whole plant in which the nest is placed. In the middle of the process the bird usually turns on its axis, a right angle, and thus the interior of the nest becomes rounded by the bird's breast. All new material is added to the inside of the nest.

At midday, then, the nest in question was a shallow saucer composed chiefly of Duranta and other twigs, dried grass, and bast. The leaves mentioned above had fallen some way below the nest, and the worsted and tissue paper had been crushed into a ball at one side of the nest.

By the evening more material, chiefly bast in bands about a quarter of an inch broad, had been added, and the nest looked almost as complete as some bulbuls' nests in which I have seen eggs. But that particular pair were evidently bent on building a very substantial structure.

By 8 a.m. on the following day the cup of the nest had grown deeper, and its walls had been considerably thickened. By the evening of the day the nest was practically complete. On the 5th March the finishing touches were put to it in the shape of a few grasses and prickly stems.

The diameter of the completed nest is between 2½ and 3 inches. The nest is rarely quite circular. It is about 2½ inches in depth. The length of its diameter appears to be determined by that of the bird's body (exclusive of head and tail) which is the mould that shapes it. A bulbul sitting in the nest looks very cramped and uncomfortable, with the tail projecting vertically upwards, the neck stretched out, and the chin resting on the rim of the nest. The crest of the sitting bird is folded right back.

On the early morning of the 8th March the first egg was laid. On the 9th a second egg was deposited. My little boy, to whom I had shown the nest, then thought that he would like a couple of bulbul's eggs poached for his breakfast, so, regardless of the feelings of the bulbuls, removed both eggs and took them to the cook! As that individual declined to cook them, my little son replaced them, or rather one of them, for he broke the other. On the morning of the 10th a third egg was laid and deposited in the nest beside the other. The usual clutch of *Otocompsa emeria* is three. On the morning of the 11th I found the nest half pulled down and empty and on the ground beneath I saw a few bulbul's feathers. Some predaceous creature, possibly a cat or a mongoose, had seized the sitting bulbul in the night.

The above notes show that a pair of bulbuls can build a nest in a couple of days. This observation was confirmed by another pair who constructed a nest in my verandah on the 23rd and 24th March. On the 22nd I noticed a pair of bulbuls prospecting in a croton plant near my *daftar* window; nevertheless, although I examined that plant carefully, I found no traces of a nest. On the next day, however, I saw that the nest had been commenced. During the three following days I had no leisure in which to look at the nest, but on the 28th I found a bulbul sitting on three eggs, so that, as only one egg per diem is laid, the first egg must have been deposited on the morning of the 26th at the latest.

On returning to my bungalow at about 10.30 p.m. of the 28th, I found some of the servants collected in the verandah. They showed me a dead brown tree snake (*Hipsas trigonata*) which they had killed in the plant containing the bulbuls' nest. The reptile had evidently discovered the nest and crawled up the stem of the plant. At its approach the incubating bulbul had made a great commotion which attracted the notice of the servants. They promptly killed the snake. On my return the eggs were lying broken on the ground, and I was not able to discover whether the fluttering bulbul or the servants striking the snake had caused their downfall. No further eggs were laid. Bulbuls seem always to desert a nest when their eggs are destroyed. It is worthy of note that the snake attacked the nest in the dark, and on all other occasions on which I have observed similar tragedies they have been enacted at night. What, then, becomes of the elaborate theory of protective colouration ?

XXIV

NIGHTINGALES IN INDIA

THE nightingale shares with the Taj Mahal the distinction of being an object on which every person lavishes high praise. All who hear the song of the nightingale go into ecstasies over it; similarly, every human being who sets eyes on the Taj waxes enthusiastic at the sight thereof. Some years ago a writer in the *Globe* stated that a patient investigator compiled a list of nearly two hundred epithets bestowed by poets alone on the nightingale's song, and I doubt not that an equally patient investigator could compile an equally long list of adjectives lavished on the Taj Mahal by those who have attempted to describe that famous tomb. The consequence is that every superlative in the English language has been appropriated by some person, so that he who nowadays wishes to bestow something original in the way of praise on either the nightingale or the Taj is at his wit's end to know what to say. Recently I met in a railway train a Portuguese gentleman who was paying a visit to India. Needless to say, I asked him what he thought of the Taj. He promptly replied: "*Le Taj, ah! c'est un bijou.*" I feel that by way of paying the necessary homage to the nightingale I cannot do better than repeat "*c'est un bijou.*"

Ornithologists assure us that there are three species of nightingale. There is the Western nightingale (*Daulias luscinia*), which visits England in the summer and fills the woods with its glorious melody. Then there is the Eastern species or variety which is also known as the sprosser (*D. philomela*), and, lastly, the Persian nightingale, the *hazar-dastan* or *bulbul* of the Persian poets. This last variety is known to men of science as *Daulias golzii*.

It would puzzle the ordinary man to distinguish between these various races. The length of the tail is one test. If the nightingale have a tail well over three inches in length it is the Persian form, if well under three inches it is a Western nightingale, and if about three inches a sprosser. The nightingale, as every one knows, is a small bird varying from 6½ to 7½ inches in length. Both sexes dress alike and in the plainest manner possible, the upper plumage being russet brown and the lower pale buff.

As we have seen, one of the Persian names of the nightingale is "bulbul." This has given rise to considerable misunderstanding regarding the existence of nightingales in India. Every one knows that India teems with bulbuls, and as "bulbul" is the Persian for nightingale, the average Englishman labours under the delusion that Hindustan abounds with nightingales which fill the soft Indian night with melody, at the time

> "When mangoes redden and the asoka buds
> Sweeten the breeze and Rama's birthday comes."

Now, as a matter of fact, the Indian bulbul has nothing whatever to do with the nightingale. There can, I think, be but little doubt that the Persian poets have misapplied the word " bulbul " in using it to denote the nightingale. The term " bulbul " is familiar to every native of India as meaning one of the Brachypodous birds belonging to the genera *Molpastes, Otocompsa,* etc., and as there are true bulbuls in Persia, one of which, *Molpastes leucotis,* is a good singer, it is probable that the poets, who are notoriously bad naturalists, have misapplied the name of this songster to an even better singer, namely, the nightingale. And this name, having been immortalised by Hafiz and others, will always remain. We must, therefore, be careful to distinguish between the true bulbuls, which are not very brilliant singers, and the nightingale, which in India is known as the *bulbul bostha*, or *bulbul basta.* Numbers of Persian nightingales are captured and sent in cages to India, where they are highly prized on account of their vocal powers. A good singing cock will fetch as much as Rs. 400 in Calcutta. The cock nightingale alone sings, and as he is indistinguishable in appearance from the hen, a would-be purchaser, before paying a long price for one of these birds, should insist on hearing it sing. Nightingales thrive in captivity if provided with a plentiful supply of insect food. The Western and Eastern forms have both bred in captivity, and the Persian variety will doubtless do likewise if given proper accommodation.

Indian bulbuls, then, are not nightingales. Nor

are nightingales common in that country. Oates, it is true, includes *Daulias golzii* among the birds of India, but, in my opinion, on insufficient evidence. He admits that it is of extreme rarity in the country, "only two instances of its occurrence being known." Hume, in October, 1865, had a Persian nightingale sent to him, which was said to have been procured in the Oudh terai. It is probable that neither this specimen nor the other whose presence is recorded in India was a wild bird at all; as likely as not they were caged birds that had escaped from captivity! The nightingale is certainly a very retiring bird, and since, if it occurs in India, it can be only as a winter visitor when it is not in song, it is possible that it might be overlooked. But in face of the fact that many good ornithologists have spent long periods in Oudh without ever having seen a nightingale, and the bird has never been observed anywhere else in India, it seems most improbable that nightingales ever stray into India. What, then, are we to think of the statement of Dr. Hartert, a German ornithologist, who says of the Eastern nightingale that "it winters in Southern Arabia, parts of India (e.g. Oudh) and East Africa"?

Here we have an excellent illustration of the adage "A little learning is a dangerous thing," a good example of how erroneous statements creep into scientific books. Dr. Hartert has heard that nightingales have been recorded in Oudh, so jumps to the conclusion that the species winters there, even as it does in Egypt. This statement will doubtless be copied, without acknowledgment, into many future text-books, for plagiarism is very rife among men of science; and thus the popular notion that nightingales are common in India will be fortified by scientific support! Nightingales undoubtedly do winter in India—but only in cages. We have many fine songsters in Hindustan, but the nightingale is not one of them.

XXV

THE WIRE-TAILED SWALLOW

WERE each species of bird to record in writing its opinion of men, the resulting document would certainly not be flattering to the human race. The inhumanity of man would figure largely in it. The majority of the feathered folk have but little cause to love their human neighbours. Men steal their eggs, destroy their nests, kill them in order to eat them or to decorate women with their plumage, and capture them in order to keep them in cages. A few species, however, ought to regard man with friendly eyes, for they owe much to him. The swallow tribe, for example, must acknowledge man as its greatest benefactor. Take the case of the common swallow (*Hirundo rustica*), the joyful herald of the English summer, the bird to which Gilbert White devotes a particularly charming letter. All the places in which this species builds owe their origin to human beings. The myriads of swallows that visit Great Britain in the spring find in the chimneys of houses ideal nesting places—hence the birds are known as house or chimney swallows.

" The swallow," writes White, " though called

the chimney swallow, by no means builds altogether in chimneys, but often within barns and outhouses against the rafters, and so she did in Virgil's time:

> 'Ante
> Garrula quam tignis nidos suspendat hirundo.'

"In Sweden she builds in barns, and is called *ladu swala*, the barn swallow. Besides, in the warmer parts of Europe there are no chimneys to houses, except they are English-built. In those countries she constructs her nest in porches and gateways and galleries and open halls. Here and there a bird may affect some odd, peculiar place, as we have known a swallow build down the shaft of an old well through which chalk had been formerly drawn up for the purpose of manure; but in general with us this *Hirundo* breeds in chimneys, and loves to haunt those stacks where there is a constant fire, no doubt for the sake of warmth. Not that it can subsist in the immediate shaft where there is a fire, but prefers one adjoining to that of the kitchen, and disregards the perpetual smoke of that funnel, as I have often observed with some degree of wonder."

In the days before man began to build substantial houses for his habitation, the swallows can have nested only in caverns and under natural ledges in cliffs, so cannot have existed in anything like their present numbers. *Hirundo rustica* is a common bird in India. During the winter it spreads itself over the plains, and may be seen, as in England, dashing through the air after tiny insects. In the East the gentle twittering of the birds as they propel themselves through the air sounds doubly sweet, since it recalls scenes in our distant island. The swallows which winter in India migrate to the Himalayas or Kashmir or Afghanistan, where they rear up their families.

But to-day I write of a more beautiful bird even than *Hirundo rustica*, of the most beautiful of the swallow kind, of a species on which Gilbert White could not have set eyes. Like the common species, the wire-tailed swallow (*Hirundo smithii*) is a glossy, steel-blue bird. The forehead, crown, and nape are chestnut, and all the lower plumage, including the chin, is white. In this last respect it differs considerably from the common swallow, which has the chin and throat chestnut, a black pectoral band, and the rest of the under parts pale reddish brown. In both species there is a white spot on each of the tail feathers, except the median pair. These white spots are very conspicuous when the bird sits with tail expanded.

The chief characteristic of *Hirundo smithii* is the great development of the shafts of the outer tail feathers. In most swallows the shaft is elongated. In *H. rustica* it extends 2½ inches beyond the other tail feathers. In the wire-tailed swallow the shaft of each of the outer tail feathers attains a length of seven inches, and is thus more than twice as long as the body of the bird. This swallow, indeed, looks as though two pieces of wire had been inserted into its tail; hence the popular name, which is far more appropriate than the scientific one. Jerdon called this species *H. filifera*, an excellent name, but among cabinet ornithologists the excellence or appropriateness of a bird's name counts for nothing. Many years ago a member of the Smith family made the acquaintance of the bird, and it was named after him. This name being the oldest is the one by which we must call the bird until some bibliophile manages to unearth some yet earlier name.

The elongated shafts of the outer tail feathers are brittle and easily broken, so that it is the exception rather than the rule to see a bird with both the delicate filiferous appendages complete.

The habits of this swallow are similar to those of other species, except that it is probably not migratory. It is found all the year round in the plains of North-West India. It is rare in Lower Bengal, Assam, Upper Burma, and in South India. Although it occurs in the Madras Presidency, it is not often seen as far south as the city of Madras. Since water is always conducive to the presence of the small insects on which swallows feed, these birds usually seek their quarry in the vicinity of the liquid element, and naturally roost near their feeding grounds. This fondness for the neighbourhood of water doubtless gave origin to the once prevalent belief that some swallows did not leave England in the autumn, but remained behind and hibernated underwater. This idea is, of course, erroneous.

Wire-tailed swallows like to roost in considerable companies in the minarets of mosques or in other lofty towers. Unlike swifts, swallows frequently perch. Telegraph wires are a very favourite resting place. When these are not available the birds will settle on stones or tufts of grass.

As chimneys are scarce in the plains of India, the wire-tailed swallow has to look elsewhere for nesting sites. True to the traditions of its family, it almost invariably elects to build on some structure erected by man. Nine out of ten nests are built under the arches of low bridges or culverts, preferably those under which there is a little water lying. The nest projects from the arch like a little shelf. It resembles a deep saucer in shape, and is composed of a shell of mud, lined with feathers.

Wire-tailed swallows obtain the mud they use from the edge of water, and carry it in the bill in precisely the same way as the house martin does in England. One of the prettiest sights of a London suburb is to watch the house martins taking the materials for their nests from a muddy road, which they always contrive to do without soiling their white-feathered legs. Muddy roads are not common in India, hence wire-tailed swallows are not able to resort to them for nest-building materials.

The cup of the nest is usually fairly thick, especially at the place where the nest is attached to its foundation. The outside of the cup has a rugged appearance, and each of the projections which it displays corresponds to a mouthful of mud added to it by the bird. According to Mr. James Aitken, the birds occupy about four weeks in building the nest, "a narrow layer of mud being added each day and left to dry."

When once a pair of wire-tailed swallows have made up their minds to nest in a certain spot they are not easily deterred from carrying out their intention. Mr. Aitken admits having on one occasion removed two eggs, out of a clutch of three, but the little mother sat on and hatched out the one egg that remained. A man of my acquaintance, who, although an egg collector, is not altogether devoid of the milk of kindness, always carries about with him one or two sparrow's eggs which he exchanges for the birds' eggs he wishes to add to his collection. One May day at Lahore this person came upon a wire-tailed swallow's nest which contained one egg. This he removed, and substituted for it a sparrow's egg. The owners of the nest either did not, or pretended not to, notice the exchange, and the hen laid two more eggs, so that when I visited the nest three days later I found that two legitimate eggs had been placed beside the spurious one. The incubating bird sat very tight, and allowed me to touch her, and had I wished to do so I could easily have caught her; such is the strength of the incubating instinct in some birds. The nest in question was built under a low arch, one end of which was blocked up. The only other occupants of the arch were a number of wasps. Birds seem to have little or no fear of wasps. Indeed, it is rather the wasps that fear the birds, which have a disagreeable habit of swallowing them, notwithstanding their sting and warning colouration! Three weeks later I paid another visit to the arch in question, and found that the swallow's nest had been removed by some person or persons unknown, but under the same arch was another nest containing two eggs. It would seem that the plucky little birds, undaunted by the fate of their first nest and eggs, had quickly set to work to make good the loss.

XXVI

WINTER VISITORS TO THE PUNJAB PLAINS

SIX months ago we welcomed the birds that came to spend the summer with us—the tiny iridescent purple sunbird, the emerald bee-eater, its larger blue-tailed cousin, the golden oriole, the superb paradise flycatcher, the yellow-throated sparrow, the solemn night heron, and the noisy koel.

These have all built their nests, reared up their families (except, of course, the koels who made the crows do their nursemaids' work) and departed. The sunbirds were the first, and the koels the last, to go. By August the former had all disappeared, but throughout the first half of October young koels were to be seen, perched in trees, flapping their wings, opening a great red mouth, and making creditable but ludicrous attempts at cawing.

Even the koels have now gone and will not reappear until the sun once again causes us human beings to wonder why we have come to this " Land of Regrets."

The places left vacant by the summer visitors are being rapidly filled up. Lahore has for birds a winter as well as a summer season. The former is the more important of the two. So numerous are our winter bird visitors that it is not feasible to enumerate them in this place; we must be content with a glimpse at those which come in the greatest numbers and are, therefore, most likely to attract attention.

The earliest to arrive are the rosy starlings (*Pastor roseus*) or *Gulabi Mainas*, or *Tilyers* as the natives call them. They are easy to recognise. They go about in great flocks. When a flock settles on a tree it is a point of etiquette for all the individuals that compose it to talk simultaneously. The head, crest, neck, throat, upper breast, wings, and tail are glossy black. The rest of the plumage is a beautiful rose colour in the adult cock and pale coffee colour in the hens and young cocks.

Rosy starlings arrive in Lahore as early as July. As they do not leave us until the end of April, and are supposed to nest in Asia Minor, it might be thought that they are the discoverers of some specially rapid method of nest-construction, egg-incubation, and bird-rearing. This is not so. The fact is they do not migrate simultaneously. The birds that were in Lahore in such numbers last April are not those which appeared in July. These latter probably migrated to Asia Minor in February.

It is only in the spring that the rosy starlings go about in very large flocks; these are the result of "packing" prior to migration. At other times the birds occur in nines and tens and associate with the ordinary mynas, feeding either on fruit or grain.

They appear to be the favourite game bird of the

native of the Punjab. They are quite good to eat. A charge of small shot fired into a tree full of them brings down a dozen or more, so that a " crack " shot is easily able to secure a large bag and brag about it to his friends!

Several other species of starling visit the plains of the Punjab during the winter, arriving in November. These, like the familiar English starling, are all dressed in black, glossed with blue, green, and purple, and spotted with white. The species-making propensity of the professional ornithologist has led to the division of these into a number of species, although it requires an expert with an ornithological imagination to distinguish them from one another. They go about in flocks and, like the rosy starlings, all " talk at once."

The winter visitors that appeal most to the sportsman are the game birds—the grey quail, the various species of duck, teal, geese, and snipe. The quail (*Coturnix communis*) are the first to appear. They arrive in Lahore late in August or early in September. It is the moon rather than the temperature that determines the date of their arrival. They migrate at night-time and naturally like to travel by moonlight. A few grey quail remain with us all the year round. These are probably birds that have been wounded by *shikaris* and have not in consequence sufficient strength for the long migratory flight across the Himalayas. The fact that some quail remain in India throughout the hot weather, and are able to breed successfully, shows that their migration is a luxury rather than a necessity.

It is a universal rule that all migratory birds of the Northern Hemisphere breed in the more northerly of their two homes. This seems to indicate that they were formerly permanent residents in the latter. Geology tells us that thousands of years ago the climate of this earth suddenly became colder. The result was that the more northerly portions of it were rendered uninhabitable for birds during the winter—the frost killed insect life and the snow made vegetable food difficult to procure; hence, the birdfolk were confronted with the alternative of starving in winter or going south in search of food. They chose the latter alternative. So powerful is the "homing instinct"—the instinct that man has developed so wonderfully in the homer pigeon—that these migrants invariably returned in the summer to their old homes for breeding purposes.

The climate has again become milder, so that for many migratory birds migration is no longer necessary; nevertheless, they still perform the double journey every year. The force of habit is strong in birds. Those Australian finches which are imported into India, even when kept in aviaries in the Himalayas, nest in December and January as they did in Australia, where these are summer months.

The ducks and geese that visit the Punjab in winter are too numerous to be dealt with in this brief essay, which of necessity is not exhaustive. It merely deals with such of the winter visitors to the Punjab as are seen every day. Every winter Northern India is invaded by millions of grey-lag and barred-headed geese, and by hundreds of thousands of brahmany ducks, mallard, gadwall, teal, wigeon, pintails, shovellers and pochards. The other game birds which visit the Punjab in great numbers every winter are the jack and the common snipe.

The Indian redstart or firetail (*Ruticilla rufiventris*) is one of the most striking of our winter visitors. No one but a blind man can fail to notice the sprightly little bird with St. Vitus' dance in its tail. The head, breast, neck, and back of the cock are grey or black according to the season of the year. Birds' clothes wear out just as ours do. But every bird is his own tailor. When his clothes wear out, instead of resorting to the West-End tailor or the humble *darzi*, he grows a new coat. This process is technically known as the moult and occurs at the end of summer in most birds.

Each of the feathers composing the coat of the cock redstart is black with a grey margin. When the feathers are new only the grey edges show, the bird, therefore, looks grey; gradually the grey borders become worn away, so that the bird turns black. The remainder of the plumage of the cock, except the two middle tail feathers, is brick red. The hen is reddish brown where the cock is black or grey. As the bird hops about in the garden it looks very like a robin, but the moment it takes to its wings it becomes transformed, as if by magic, into a flash of red. The red of the tail and back is scarcely visible when the bird is not flying, for the wings cover the latter and the tail is closed like a fan; the red feathers all folding up underneath the middle brown ones which act as a cover. During flight the red tail feathers open out and the wings leave the red back exposed—hence the sudden transformation.

The redstart should be a favourite with Englishmen, because in habits and appearance it resembles the familiar robin of our country. The perverse Indian robin (*Thamnobia cambayensis*), it will be remembered, insists on wearing its patch of red, as Phil Robinson hath it, on the seat of its trousers.

The Indian redstart arrives towards the end of September. In the autumn of 1906, September 22nd was the date on which I first noticed a redstart in Lahore. In the following autumn I did not see one until September 27th. Bird-lovers of fixed abode in India would be rendering no small service to ornithology if they would record carefully, year after year, the dates on which they first observe each of our returning summer and winter visitors.

When the migrant wagtails arrive we feel that the hot weather is really over. Three species of wagtail are common in Lahore. One of these—the pied wagtail (*Motacilla maderaspatensis*)—is a permanent resident. The other two—the white wagtail (*Motacilla alba*) and the grey wagtail (*M. melanope*)—come to us only for the winter. The last is easily distinguished by its bright yellow lower plumage. The white and the pied wagtails are both clothed in black and white, but whereas the face and throat of the former are white, the whole head of the pied wagtail is black save for a white eye-brow.

Wagtails live almost entirely on the ground. Throughout the winter dozens of them are to be seen on the gymkhana cricket ground, sprinting after tiny insects, and stopping after each capture to indulge in a little tail wagging. All three species of wagtail feed exclusively on insects, so that the migration in this case, as in that of the quail and of many other birds, is obviously due to the force of habit.

Another winter visitor that cannot fail to attract attention is the white-eared bulbul (*Molpastes leucotis*), a bird loathed by the gardener on account of the damage it does to buds.

Two species of bulbul are abundant in Lahore: this one and the Punjab red-vented bulbul (*Molpastes intermedius*). The latter, like the poor, is always with us, while the former shakes the dust of Lahore off its feet and departs when the weather becomes hot. The permanent resident has a red patch under its tail and a black head and crest, while the migrant wears yellow under the tail and has white cheeks.

The family of birds of prey furnishes us with a large number of winter visitors. Those most likely to be seen in the neighbourhood of Lahore are the steppe eagle, the long-legged buzzard, the sparrow hawk, the peregrine falcon, the kestrel, and the merlin. It must not be thought that *all* our Indian birds of prey are migrants. A number of species remain in the plains throughout the hot weather to vex the souls of their weaker brethren. Curiously enough, there is among the permanently resident raptores a counterpart, a nearly allied species—I might almost say a "double" —of nearly every migrant. The tawny eagle (*Aquila vindhiana*) and the steppe eagle (*A. bifasciata*) are so alike that some authorities are inclined to regard them as a single species. But the former lives in the plains all the year round and breeds in and about Lahore, while the steppe eagle goes to the hills in the hot weather to breed, and appears quite unable to endure heat. The one caught at Wazirabad in the cold weather of 1906–7 and confined in the local "Zoo" died comparatively early in the hot weather, whereas the tawny eagle, kept in the same cage, has all along flourished like the green bay tree. The shikra (*Astur badius*) and the sparrow hawk (*Accipiter nisus*), although ornithologists now place them in different genera, are so much alike that it is easy to mistake one for the other, yet the former is a permanent resident while the latter is a migrant. Similarly the peregrine falcon (*Falco peregrinus*) is a winter visitor to the plains of the Punjab, while its cousin the laggar (*Falco jugger*) is a permanent resident. In the same way the *Turumti* or red-headed merlin abides with us all the year round, while the common merlin (*Aesalon regulus*) visits us only in winter.

Almost the only raptorial winter visitor that has not a cousin who lives in the plains throughout the year is the kestrel (*Tinnunculus alaudarius*), the bird known in England as the Windhover. This is perhaps the easiest to identify of all the birds of prey, on account of its habit of hovering on vibrating wings, like the pied kingfisher, high in the air, over a spot where it thinks that there is quarry in the shape of some small rodent. If the surmise be correct the kestrel drops like a stone and seizes its quarry in its talons; if it sees nothing it sweeps away with a few easy movements of its powerful wings and hovers elsewhere. The only other bird of prey that hovers like the kestrel is the black-winged kite (*Elanus caerulus*). This is mainly white and so cannot be confounded with the kestrel.

The explanation of the fact that one species of bird of prey leaves the plains in the hot weather, while a nearly related species remains, may perhaps be found in the nature of their food. Birds of prey are to a greater or lesser extent specialists; while quite ready to devour any small bird, reptile, or mammal which comes their way, they lay themselves out more especially to catch one particular species, and if that species migrates it follows that the bird that preys upon it will also migrate. Thus the peregrine falcon lays itself out to catch ducks and naturally goes with them to their breeding grounds, just as the hawker of cheap wares, who preys upon the *mem-sahib*, follows her to the hills in the summer.

In conclusion mention must be made of the *Corvi* which visit us in winter. The arch-corvus, the grey-necked rascal (*Corvus splendens*), of course, abides with us all the year round. The raven, too, is to be seen at all times of the year, but is more abundant in the cold weather than in the hot. During the summer months we see comparatively few ravens; in the winter they are exceedingly numerous. Every evening towards sunset a long stream of them may be observed flying in a westerly direction to the common roosting place. There is a similar stream of crows that flies in a north-westerly direction. The rook (*Corvus frugilegus*) is a permanent resident of Kashmir and the North-Western Himalayas, but in mid-winter many individuals are driven by the cold into the Frontier Province and the Punjab; some come as far south as Lahore, where they consort with the crows. If the winter is a severe one large numbers of rooks come to Lahore, otherwise these birds are not very numerous. The same applies to the jackdaw (*Corvus monedula*), but he never comes in such numbers as the rook. There is in the octagonal bird house in the Lahore "Zoo" a compartment in which there is a "Happy Family" of ravens, rooks, and jackdaws, with an Australian crow-shrike and a Nicobar pigeon to keep them company. Thus every one who cannot already do so may learn to identify the various *Corvi* which visit Lahore in the winter.

XXVII

A KINGFISHER AND A TERN

NEARLY every village in India has its pond which becomes filled with water during the monsoon and grows drier and drier during the winter and hot weather. The pond is usually a natural depression, sometimes enlarged and deepened by human agency. Occasionally a village is situated on the edge of a lake, or *jhil,* but such fortunate villages are few and far between ; the average hamlet has to be content with a small tank. This morning I came upon such a tank, in which the water had become low, leaving a wide margin of mud between it and the artificially made bank. At one end a couple of people were squatting. *Mirabile dictu,* there was not a paddy bird to be seen, and the only feathered creature disporting itself along the edge was a grey wagtail. In mid pond four domestic ducks were feeding. A tern—the Indian river tern (*Sterna seena*)—was busy at the tank, flying gracefully over the water and dipping into it every few seconds. Judging from the frequency with which the bird dived, the water must have teemed with food, but there were no signs of fish rising, so that how the eye of the tern was able to penetrate the very muddy water is a mystery. However, the tern did manage to distinguish its quarry, for, although its movements were so rapid that I was not able to discover what it was catching, I could see distinctly that, when rising, it carried something tiny in its bill.

Terns are especially addicted to pieces of water that are rapidly drying up, for under such conditions they find the creatures upon which they prey literally jostling one another. After the water has been run off from a canal, dozens of terns congregate at each hollow in the canal-bed in which water lies.

The tern, when it plunges after its quarry, takes great care not to wet its wings. Its habit is to drop from a height of about twenty feet head foremost. In the course of the plunge the head and body are often submerged, but, I think, never the wings; during the operation, these are held almost vertically. So assiduously was this tern plying his profession that he made thirty dives in about six minutes.

While he was thus employed a pied kingfisher (*Ceryle rudis*) appeared on the scene and took up a position on one of three neem trees that grew beside the tank. After sitting thus for a few seconds, he too began to seek for food. Save that both he and the tern drop from a height of about twenty feet into the water after their quarry, there is but little similarity between their movements. The tern sails gracefully along on pinions which move but slowly, while the kingfisher flies a little way, then remains stationary in the air for a few seconds on rapidly vibrating wings, with both tail and bill pointing downwards, so that the shape of the bird is an inverted V with the apex at the neck. It then either dives or passes on to another spot where it again hovers. Frequently it makes as if it were going to dive, then seems to change its mind, for it checks itself during its drop and passes on.

When the kingfisher was hovering in the air, the tern approached and looked as though he were going to attack him. However, he contented himself by skimming past very close to the "pied fish tiger." This appeared to disconcert the latter, who went back to the neem tree and rested there for a few minutes. Meanwhile, the tern flew away. The moment he had departed the kingfisher renewed his piscatorial efforts and took up a position about twenty feet above the water almost directly over the spot where the ducks were floating. I thought this rather foolish on the part of the kingfisher, because the ducks must necessarily scare away all the fish from that part of the water. However, the little fisherman possessed more sense than I gave him credit for. He had not been hovering for thirty seconds when he plunged into the water and emerged with a large object in his bill. With this he flew to the muddy border of the pond. Then, by means of my field glasses, I saw that his quarry consisted of a frog about two and a half inches long including the legs. The kingfisher experienced some little difficulty in swallowing the frog. He had it crosswise in his beak and the problem that confronted him was to get the frog lengthwise head foremost in his bill without releasing the nimble little amphibian and thus giving it a chance of escape. After a little manœuvring the kingfisher got the frog in the desired position, and, having held it thus for a few seconds, swallowed it.

Then the kingfisher remained squatting on the bank for a couple of minutes looking pensive. This was scarcely to be wondered at, seeing that as regards size the frog bore to him the same relation as a large mackerel does to a man. I was interested to see whether the kingfisher would consider this a sufficient meal, or whether he would immediately resume his fishing operations. I expected him to adopt the latter course, for birds have most voracious appetites. If horses were to eat in the same ratio they would require at least a maund of oats per diem to keep them in health! My surmise was correct. In a few seconds the kingfisher flew to a large stake projecting from the water and squatted there, cocking up his tail at frequent intervals. This motion of the tail is possibly an aid to digestion! When he was thus seated, the tern reappeared on the scene and at once recommenced fishing in the manner already described. After the tern had been fishing for a couple of minutes the kingfisher resumed operations and again sought the neighbourhood of the ducks. He soon captured a second frog; but this time, instead of being able to bear it to the bank and devour it in peace, he had to reckon with the tern. He had not risen a yard above the water when the tern noticed that he had quarry. Forthwith the tern committed a breach of the tenth commandment and then proceeded to try to violate the eighth. He made a swoop at the kingfisher, which the latter adroitly dodged, squeaking loudly but without dropping the frog. Then ensued a chase which was a sight for the gods. As regards pace on the wing the kingfisher is no match for the tern. In an aerial contest the slower flier has the advantage of being able to twist and turn more quickly than the rapid flier. Of this advantage the kingfisher availed itself to the full, so that the contest waxed fast and furious, the combatants moving in a series of curves, zigzags, circles, and other geometrical figures.

The kingfisher, notwithstanding that he had just swallowed a frog, evidently had not the least intention of delivering up his catch. The tern appeared equally determined to capture it. Seeing that he would never be able to enjoy the fruits of his prowess while he remained at the tank, the kingfisher changed his tactics and flew right away, disappearing behind some trees, with the tern in pursuit. The latter, however, did not follow far. He seemed suddenly to come to the conclusion that honesty is the best policy, and returned to the pond to endeavour to secure food in a more legitimate manner. I waited on for about half an hour, expecting to see the kingfisher reappear, but was disappointed. Then the tern went to seek pastures new, and left the ducks and a solitary wagtail in possession of the tank.

XXVIII

THE RED TURTLE DOVE

INSECTS and birds, on account of the vast number of species they present, furnish the best available material for the study of evolution. It is owing to the fact that most Professors of Zoology are neither entomologists nor ornithologists that biological science is in its present deplorably backward condition. There exists scarcely a zoological theory, be it neo-Lamarckian or neo-Darwinian, that the competent ornithologist is not able to refute. For example, writing of sexual dimorphism in animals, Cunningham states that in the case of birds which exhibit such dimorphism the cocks differ essentially in habits from the hens, and in this way he, as a Lamarckian, would account for their external differences. "The cocks of common fowls and of the *Phasianidæ* generally," he writes, "are polygamous, fight with each other for the possession of females, and take no part in incubation or care of the young, and they differ from the hens in their enlarged brilliant plumage, spurs on the legs, and combs, wattles, or other excrescences on the head. In the *Columbidæ, per contra*, the males are not polygamous, but pair for life, the males do not fight, and share equally with the females in parental duties. Corresponding with the contrast of sexual habits is the contrast of sexual dimorphism, which is virtually absent in the *Columbidæ*."

Mr. Cunningham evidently is not acquainted with the red turtle dove (*Œnopopelia tranqebarica*) so common in India, or he would not have asserted that sexual dimorphism is virtually absent in the *Columbidæ*. The sexes in this species are very different in appearance, and I know of nothing peculiar in its habits to explain this dissimilarity. The sexual dimorphism displayed by the red turtle dove is a fact equally awkward for the Wallaceians, because the habits of this species appear to be in no way different from those of the other doves. I have seen red turtle doves feeding in company with the three other common species of Indian dove; they eat the same kind of food, build the same ramshackle nests, and lay the usual white eggs. But I will not spend time in whipping a dying horse. The poor overburdened beast which we call Natural Selection has done yeoman service; for years he has pulled the great car of Zoology along the rugged road of knowledge, and now that he is past work, now that he stands tugging impotently at the traces, it is time to pension him and replace him by a new steed. Unfortunately, the drivers of the coach happen to be old gentlemen, so old that they fail to perceive that the coach is at a standstill. They believe that they are still travelling along as merrily as they were in Darwin's time. Ere long their seats will be occupied by new drivers, who will give the good steed Natural Selection a well-earned rest, and replace him by a fresh animal called Mutation. Then once again the coach will resume its journey.

The red turtle dove is a little bird, and the hen looks like an exceptionally small specimen of the ring dove. So great is the resemblance that a hen red turtle dove was shown at the United Provinces Exhibition at Allahabad as a ring dove. The cock red turtle dove has a pretty grey head, a black half-collar running round the back of his neck, which, as Jerdon remarks, is "well set off by whitish above," while the remainder of his upper plumage is dull brick red. The hen is clothed in greyish brown, in the hue known as dove colour, and her one ornament is a black half-collar similar to that of the cock.

The best friends of turtle doves can scarcely maintain that they have melodious voices. Phil Robinson, writing of the species which visits England, contrasts its note with the "mellow voluptuous cooing of the ring-dove." "The call of the turtle dove," he says, "is unamiable, usually grumbling, and often absolutely disagreeable. To the imagination it is a sulky and discontented bird, perpetually finding fault with its English surroundings of foliage, weather, and food. 'Do, for goodness' sake get those eggs hatched, my dear, and let us get back to Italy.' That is the burden of his grumble, morning, noon, and night."

Phil Robinson's opinion of the call of the red turtle dove is not on record; this is unfortunate, for, assuredly, it would be a document worthy to be placed side by side with Mr. Lloyd George's invective against the House of Lords!

To describe the note of the turtle dove as a coo would be to violate the truth. It is a sepulchral grunt, the kind of sound one might expect of a ring dove suffering from an acute sore throat. The only other bird which makes a noise in any way resembling the call of the turtle dove is an owl that makes itself heard in India shortly after the shades of night have fallen. To what species this owl belongs I know not, for it is no easy matter to fix on the owner of a voice heard only after dark, and the descriptions of the cries of the various owls given in ornithological works are anything but illuminating. The owl in question is, I think, the brown fish owl (*Ketupa ceylonsis*), but of this I am not certain.

The red turtle dove occurs throughout India, but, as in the case of the other species of dove, its distribution appears to be capricious. It is a permanent resident in the United Provinces, and, possibly, in South India, although I am inclined to think that it goes north to breed. Of this I am not sure. It never does to be sure of anything connected with doves; they are most unreliable birds. To give a concrete instance. Having lived for two years at Lahore, and having seen any number of red turtle doves there during the hot weather, but not even the shadow of one in the cold season, I was rash enough to assert in a scientific journal: "There is no doubt that this species is merely a summer visitor to Lahore." As if to stultify me, some red turtle doves took into their heads to remain on in Lahore during the following winter, and at the end of September, when they ought to have been far away, a pair of them were hatching out eggs. On the 27th of that month Mr. Currie found a nest containing three fresh eggs. The laying of three eggs was an additional piece of effrontery on the part of the lady turtle dove, and she was rewarded by having them captured by Mr. Currie. As every one knows, two is the correct number of eggs for a respectable pair of doves. I have found dozens of doves' nests, but have never seen more than two eggs in any of them. Two is the normal number for the red turtle dove, but this species has a trick of occasionally laying three, and so would seem to be departing from the traditions of the family in the matter of egg-laying.

As regards architecture, it has not made any advances on the vulgar herd of doves. Its nursery is the typical slight structure over which so many ornithologists have waxed sarcastic—a few slender sticks, or pieces of grass, or both, so loosely and sparsely put together that the eggs can generally be spied from below through the bottom of the nest. Hume states that he has always found the nest at or near the extremities of the lower branches of very large trees, at heights of from eight to fifteen feet from the ground. My experience agrees with Hume's in that the nests are placed in tall trees, but all those that I have observed have been situated high up in the tree at a level not less than twenty feet above the ground. Mr. Currie states that the nests he found at Lahore in May and June were also in high trees, forty or fifty feet from the ground, but that the nests which he found in August and September of the individuals who elected to winter at Lahore were placed in bushes or low trees, and were not more than twelve feet above the earth, one of them being at an elevation of but four feet.

XXIX

BIRDS IN THE MILLET FIELDS

THE fields of *bajra*, or giant millet, which in late autumn or early winter form so conspicuous a feature of the landscape of Northern India, are a never-failing source of amusement to the naturalist, because they are so attractive to the feathered folk. Were the bird visitors asked why they came to the *bajra*, they would doubtless reply, if they could speak, that the attraction was the insects harboured by the crops. And the majority would be telling the truth. But there are, alas, some who come for a less useful purpose, that of abstracting the grain. Let us deal first with the avian black sheep. Of these, the buntings are the most numerous, unless the particular field happens to be within a mile of a village; in that case, of course, the sparrows outnumber them. On *Passer domesticus* I have not leisure to dwell. It must suffice that he eats and twitters and squabbles to his heart's content all day long, and generally enjoys himself at the expense of the cultivator.

The buntings merit more attention. They are aristocratic connections of the sparrow. They need no introduction to the Englishman, for of their clan is the yellow-hammer, the little bird that sits on a fence and calls cheerily "A little bit of bread and no che-e-e-se." Like other grain-eating birds, buntings possess a stout bill—not a coarse beak like that of the bullfinch or even of the sparrow, but a powerful, conical, sharply pointed instrument with which they are able to extract grain from the ear and then husk it preparatory to swallowing it. A peculiarity of the bill of the bunting is that the upper and lower mandibles do not come into contact along their whole length, but are separated in the middle by a gap which gives the beak the appearance of having been used to crack grain too hard for it.

Fifteen species of bunting visit India. I am not going to attempt to describe all these, for two excellent reasons. The first is that no one would read my descriptions, and the second is that I have never set eyes upon several of the Indian buntings. Three species, however, are very abundant, and one fairly so, in Northern India, during the cold weather. Buntings are not often seen south of Bombay. As they find plenty of grain in northern latitudes, there is no necessity for them to penetrate into the tropics. The grey-necked, the red-headed and the black-headed are the three commonest species. The grey-necked bunting (*Emberiza buchanani*) is an ashy-brown bird with a reddish tinge in its lower plumage, and a whitish ring round the eye. It is a bird that is apt to pass unnoticed unless looked for. This perhaps explains why Oates wrongly states that the species is not found east of Etawah. The cock red-headed bunting (*E. luteola*) is a handsome bird, nor has the hen any reason to be ashamed of her appearance, whatever the ladies of the other species may say. The wings and tail of the cock are greenish brown. His head is a beautiful old-gold colour, while his rump and lower parts are bright yellow. In the hen the colouring is everywhere more subdued. In the cock black-headed bunting (*E. melanocephala*) the feathers that adorn the head are black with a grey border, so that the head looks grey when the bird first reaches India in the autumn, but grows blacker as the grey edges of the feathers become worn away. The back and shoulders are rich chestnut, the wings and tail are brown, the cheeks and lower plumage rich yellow. The hen is brownish with dull yellow under parts, and a bright yellow patch under the tail. This species, which might at a casual glance be mistaken for a weaver bird (*Ploceus baya*), is very abundant on the Bombay side, where, to quote "Eha," it "about takes the place of the yellow-hammer at home, swarming about fields and hedges, and singing with more cheer than music."

The fourth species of bunting has been promoted to a different genus because it boasts of a conspicuous crest, not unlike that of the crested lark (*Galerita cristata*). Its scientific name is *Melophus melanicterus*, and its non-scientific, or popular, or vulgar name is the crested bunting. The cock is a greyish black bird with russet-brown wings. The hen is a dark brown bird. This is said to be a resident species in the plains, whereas the other three are migratory. Otherwise its habits are very like those of the ordinary buntings. These birds spend the day in the fields. As they live in the midst of plenty they enjoy much leisure. This they employ perched on a head of millet making a joyful noise. Sometimes one will be sitting thus on a particular stalk when a friend will fly up, drive him from his position, and in turn hold forth, only to be playfully ousted by another of his comrades. Verily the life of a bunting is a jolly one.

Like rosy starlings, the buntings are not very much in evidence until they begin to collect in huge flocks preparatory to leaving India for the hot weather. Then it is impossible to miss seeing them. At that season golden corn takes the place of millet in the fields. Heavy is the toll which the buntings levy on the ripening grain. When disturbed, they take refuge in the nearest tree, and the moment the fear of danger is past they are back again in the field. Hence Jerdon calls them corn buntings.

The other black sheep of the *bajra* field are the rosy starlings (*Pastor roseus*) and the green parrots (*Palæornis torquatus*). For noisiness and destructiveness these are a pair of species hard to beat.

Having considered the sinners, it now behoves us to turn to the saints. Fortunately for the long-suffering ryot, the latter outnumber the former; the majority of the avian *habitués* of the millet field come for the sake of the insects which are so abundant in this particular crop. The most conspicuous of these is the Indian roller (*Coracias indica*), who uses the heads of the millet as convenient perches whence he can descend upon his quarry. It is not by any means every millet stalk that is sufficiently stout to support so weighty a bird, and it is amusing to watch a "blue jay" try in vain to find a perch on several successive heads, on each occasion almost losing his balance. For this reason the roller always selects for his watch-tower a castor-oil plant, when any of these are interspersed among the millet.

King-crows are always in force on the millet field, but is there any spot in India where they are not in force? They, like the roller, use the heads as resting places whence to secure their quarry, but they take it in the air in preference to picking it from off the ground.

On the highest stalk of the field sits a butcher bird, still and grim, waiting for a victim. Though he is small, you cannot fail to notice him on account of his conspicuous white shirt front. As a rule, there are no thorny bushes in the vicinity of the millet field, so that here he must devour his food without spitting it on a thorn.

Every millet field is visited by flocks of mynas—bank, pied, and common mynas—with now and then a starling. These, I believe, visit the field mainly for insects; but I would not like to assert that they do not sometimes pilfer the grain. In any case, they are a cheery crowd, and without them the *bajra* fields would not be the lively spots they are. Mention must also be made of the Indian bush chat (*Pratincola maura*)

—most unobtrusive of little birds. The hen is dressed in reddish brown, and, when apart from her lord and master, it is scarcely possible to distinguish her from several other lady chats, unless, of course, the observer be so ungallant as to shoot her. The upper parts of the cock are reddish brown in winter, black in summer. There is a large patch of white on each side of the neck. The breast is orange red, the lower parts russet brown. But what with the young cocks assuming gradually the full adult plumage, and the adults changing from the plumage of one season to that of the next, no two of these birds seem to be exactly alike. The bush chats feed upon the small insects that live on the millet plants.

Lastly, mention must be made of various species of pipits and warblers, who feed on insects down in the depths of the millet field.

Such, then, are the principal of the *dramatis personæ* of the gay little scene that is enacted daily in the millet field. But, stay—I have forgotten a very important class of personages—the birds of prey. In India these are, of course, very numerous, and many of them, more especially the harriers, habitually hunt over open fields, gliding on outstretched wings a few yards above the crops, ready to swoop down upon any creature that has failed to mark their approach. Great is the commotion among the birds in the millet when a harrier appears on the scene. The voices of the smaller birds are suddenly hushed, and their owners drop on to the ground, where they are hidden from view by the crop. The mynas, uttering harsh cries of anger, take to their wings and fly off to right and to left of the path of the harrier, as though they were soldiers performing a manœuvre. Thus the bird of prey flies over a field which is apparently devoid of living creatures. But long before he is out of sight the little birds have again come to the surface, the mynas have returned, and all are feeding as merrily as before. So cautious are the smaller birds that even a dove flying overhead causes them to drop into the depths of the crop. They do not wait to see the nature of the living object—to do so might mean death.

It may perhaps be thought that, if birds are thus in constant fear of being devoured, their life must be fraught with anxiety. Far from it. Birds know not what death is. Instinct teaches them to avoid birds of prey, but they probably enjoy the sudden dash for cover. The smaller fry appear to look upon the raptorial bird in much the same light as children regard the "bogey man." For some unknown reason, they are afraid of him, but at the same time he affords them a certain amount of amusement.

XXX

HOOPOES AT THE NESTING SEASON

UK-UK-UK—soft and clear; *uk-uk-uk*—gentle and monotonous pipes the nodding hoopoe with splendid pertinacity throughout the month of February. This is the prelude to nesting operations. From mid-February till mid-March hoopoes' eggs to the number of several millions are laid annually in India. During the months of March and April considerably over a million hoopoes emerge from the egg. In Northern India during the month of April it is scarcely possible to find an adult hoopoe who is not employed from sunrise to sunset in digging insects out of the ground with feverish haste and flying with them to the holes in which the youngsters are calling lustily.

But let me begin at the beginning. Ordinarily the Indian hoopoe (*Upupa indica*) is as sedate and prim as a maiden lady of five-and-fifty summers. At the season of courtship the hoopoes cast aside their primness to some extent. But even at that festive time the cock does not, like the king-crow and the roller, disturb the whole neighbourhood by his noisy love songs. In his wildest moments his voice is never loud.

Sometimes he chases his mate on the wing, and then the pair of lovers perform the most wonderful gyrations, twisting, turning, and doubling with greater rapidity and ease than the most mobile butterfly. The chase over, the birds descend to the ground and remain motionless for a little. Then the cock—it is impossible to distinguish the sexes by outward appearance, but it is the custom to attribute all matrimonial advances to the cock, hence I say the cock—opens out his beautiful cinnamon-and-black corona and runs rapidly along the ground. The lady of his choice pays no attention whatever to his display.

Mark this statement, gentle and ungentle readers! Mark it with a black mark, because it is an example of that horrid heterodoxy of mine which causes the worthy reviewers of a number of influential and highly respectable newspapers to indulge at intervals in much gnashing of teeth and to roar with impotent rage. The orthodox view is, of course, that the lady only pretends that she does not see the display of the cock; in reality she is watching it carefully out of the corner of her eye, and is thoroughly appreciating it. Says she to herself (according to the orthodox view), "My eye! Hasn't John James got a magnificent crest! But I must not let him know that I think it, otherwise he will suffer from swelled head and be positively unbearable to live with!"

The orthodox would have us believe that the lady hoopoe is a consummate actress. She may be. But, I submit that the burden of proof is on those who make such assertions. If the hen looks as though she is taking no notice, it is proper to assume that she is taking no notice until we can prove that this assumption is incorrect. Now, I submit that it is not possible to adduce one jot or tittle of proof of the hen's alleged pretence. All the evidence goes to show that the hen bird really does not notice the display of the cock. I ask, why should the hen dissimulate ? Why should she show without hesitation her feelings on all occasions that call for a display of feeling except this one ?

I ask again, even if the hen does notice the display of the cock, has she any sense of beauty ? Is it likely that a bird, which lays its eggs in a dirty dark hole and squats in that hole for a fortnight until it stinketh in such a manner as to be perceptible to the Indian coolie, appreciates the beauty of the corona of the cock or of the bold black-and-white markings on his wings ? I decline to attribute to the hen hoopoe all the wiles of a human coquette. But, grant that she does possess them. What of the cock ? Is he supposed to see through them ? If not, why does he display his beauties to a lady who appears persistently to refuse to notice them ? I submit that the orthodox view of the nuptial display is totally wrong. The cock does not try to show off, nor does his display win him a mate. At the breeding season the sight of the hen excites him, and his excitement shows itself in the form of dance, of the erection of certain feathers, or of song. Even as a man's joy often finds expression in song or dance, so does the pleasure of a bird. A fighting dove often goes through the antics we associate with courtship. These antics are merely the expression of excitement, and not made deliberately to attract a hen or alarm an enemy.

So much for conjecture. Let us now turn to facts. The hoopoe usually lays its eggs in a hole in a tree or a building; on rare occasions only, in a crevice of a rock or under a large stone. The most approved nesting site is a roomy cavity, as dark and dirty as possible, with a very small opening leading to the world without.

I have no wish to exaggerate, and I believe that I am understating facts when I say that I have seen more than fifty hoopoes' nests.

These have all been in cavities in trees or buildings opening to the exterior by a very small aperture. I think I may safely assert that forty-nine out of every fifty hoopoes' nests are in such situations. I emphasise this point in order to demonstrate the kind of nonsense that finds its way into English periodicals.

In the issue of the *Fortnightly Review* for February, 1912, an article by Mr. Philip Oyler appeared entitled "Colour Meanings of some British Birds and Quadrupeds."

Mr. Oyler is a disciple of that eccentric artist, Mr. Abbot Thayer, who imagines that all birds and beasts are invisible in their natural surroundings.

Mr. Oyler's article in the *Fortnightly Review* is composed chiefly of erroneous statements, wild guesses, and absurd interpretations of facts. The climax of nonsense is reached by Mr. Oyler when he writes about the hoopoe:—

"As it nests in hollow stems, and hollow stems

mean decay, there is invariably fungus on those stems. And how wonderfully the hoopoe's white copies them, and how wonderfully the black represents shadows; and then again, in addition to colouration, is a crest to help break the outline."

For the benefit of those who have not visited India I may state that in the greater part of the plains the trunks of old trees are not covered with fungus. Practically every hoopoe nests in a place completely hidden from the outer world. If the hen hoopoe were coloured with all the colours of the spectrum she would while sitting on her eggs be invisible from the outer world. It is sad to think that people exist who can bring themselves to write such nonsense as Mr. Oyler has inflicted on the readers of the *Fortnightly Review*.

It is said that a pair of hoopoes uses the same nest year after year. I have not been able to verify this statement owing to the demands on my peripatetic capacity made by the exigencies of the public service.

The eggs of the hoopoe are elongated ovals of a dirty white colour; euphemists describe them as dingy olive-brown or green, while euphuists portray them as having a delicate greyish blue tint. They are devoid of markings.

The clutch is said to contain from four to seven eggs. This is another assertion which I have never attempted to verify, because in order to reach the eggs of the hoopoe one has usually to pull down part of a wall or other edifice and at the same time wreck the nest. However, I can say that I have never observed more than two young hoopoes emerge from a nest, and on several occasions I have noticed that only one issued forth.

As concrete instances are more interesting than generalities I propose in what follows to give an account of the nesting operations of a pair of hoopoes that recently reared up a youngster in a chink in the wall of my verandah at Fyzabad between a wooden rafter and the brickwork. The cavity in question was so situated that I could see its orifice as I sat at my dressing table. I noticed for the first time a hoopoe bringing food to the nest on the 17th March. The food brought appeared to consist chiefly of caterpillars. Whenever the bird arrived at the nest it uttered a soft, pretty, tremulous *coo-coo-coo*. This was to inform its mate that it had come.

The hen hoopoe is said not to leave the nest from the time she begins to incubate until the young emerge from the eggs. This statement is, I believe, correct. It is not one that can be very easily verified because the sexes are alike in outward appearance. Certain it is that the hen sits very closely and the cock continually brings food to her.

As soon as the young are hatched out the hen leaves the nest and assists the cock in finding food for the baby hoopoes. I cannot say on what day the particular hen whose doings are here recorded left the nest. April 9th was the first date on which I noticed both birds feeding the young. At that period the parents were bringing food faster than the occupant of the nest could dispose of it, and one or other of them had often to wait outside with something in the beak until the nestling was ready to receive it. At that time I had no idea how many young birds were inside the nest. The chink that led to it was too narrow to admit of the insertion of one's hand. It was not until the young bird emerged that I discovered that only one nestling had been reared.

While the parent was thus waiting outside with a succulent caterpillar hanging from its bill, it used to utter its call *uk-uk-uk*. Sometimes while one bird was thus waiting the other would appear. Then the first bird would transfer the quarry to its mate, and the latter would either devour it or wait outside the nest with the morsel.

Most birds when they feed their young collect several organisms in the beak between the visits to the nest. Not so the hoopoe; it brings but one thing at a time, which it carries at the extreme tip of the bill. The reasons for this departure from the usual practice are obvious. The long bill of the hoopoe, like that of the snipe, is a probe to penetrate the earth. During this operation any food already in the bill would be torn and damaged. Moreover, if the hoopoe were to carry the food to the nest in the angle of the beak as most birds do, it would be difficult to transfer this to the long bill of the young bird. Hence it comes to pass that hoopoes visit their nestlings a very great number of times in the course of the day.

When young hoopoes emerge from the egg they are silent creatures, but before they are many days old they begin to welcome with squeaks the arrival of the parents with food. The older the young birds grow the more vociferous they become.

Like the majority of birds that nestle in holes, hoopoes with young display but little fear of man. The nest of which I write was situated over the door of the pantry, where servants work during the greater part of the day. The hoopoes did not seem to object at all to the presence of the servants, but they took great exception to my arrival. Whenever I came upon the scene the parent hoopoes used to greet me with a harsh *chur* uttered with crest folded back and tail expanded.

One day a corby (*Corvus macrorhynchus*), who doubtless had done to death many a promising nestling, alighted on a table placed in the verandah outside the pantry. The hoopoes were furious at the intrusion. They took up positions, to right and to left of the crow, at a safe distance, and scolded it with great vehemence. The crow took no notice whatever of this hostile demonstration. After a little one of the hoopoes flew to the ground, and from there continued its abuse of the crow. Then, while waiting to regain its breath, it expanded its crest and repeatedly bobbed its head so that the tip of the bill almost touched the ground. This bowing performance is evidently an expression of great excitement. I have seen doves behaving in a similar manner in the midst of a fight, and also when courting. Here, then, we have a case of what is usually considered to be showing off or display to the female, taking place at a time when a bird is very angry. The hoopoe in question was not showing off either to the crow or to its mate; it was assuredly no time, "no matter for his swellings nor his turkey cocks."

On the 25th April the young hoopoe began to call even when its parents were not at the nest. Each time they brought food it uttered a series of squeaks much like those that emanate from a cycle pump when air is being pumped through it into a nearly fully inflated tyre. By this time the young bird had developed to such an extent that when a parent arrived it would push its head through the aperture of the nest hole.

On the 26th April the young bird left the nest. Assuming that the 17th March was the day when the hen began to sit, we find the young bird emerging from the nest forty days later. It is, however, improbable that I noticed the cock feeding the hen on the very first day of incubation. It is my belief that young hoopoes do not leave the nest for fully a month after they are hatched. When they do leave the nest they differ very little in appearance from the adult. They have the crest and the colouring fully developed. The only difference is that the bill is not quite so long or so curved.

From the time the bird emerges from the nest until the moment when it is gathered unto its fathers, the hoopoe's plumage does not undergo any change in appearance. This being so I am puzzled to know what a correspondent meant when he recently wrote to the *Field* about a hoopoe in full breeding plumage that appeared in Yorkshire.

But let us return to the young hoopoe that emerged from the nest in my verandah at Fyzabad on the 26th April, 1912. Not content with thrusting its head and shoulders through the aperture at the visit of its father or mother as it had been doing for some time, it suddenly came right out on to the beam to meet its food-laden parent. After it had eaten the proffered caterpillar and the parent had left, the young bird caught sight of me. Immediately it opened out its crest and began bowing in the manner described above as betokening excitement. Then it fluttered on to a ledge at the distance of six feet. A minute later it flew out of the verandah and alighted on a creeper growing on a wall fifteen yards away. Its flight was wonderfully strong, but I noticed that it was breathing heavily after it had alighted, showing that the short flight entailed considerable exertion. It appeared to dislike the interest I was taking in it, and so flew on to the roof of the bungalow, where I lost sight of it.

These little incidents are, I submit, utterly subversive of the anthropomorphic theory, so much in favour nowadays and expounded by Mr. Walter Long in that much-read book *The School of the Woods*, that birds and beasts are born with their minds a blank, and that they have to be taught how to walk and how to fly just as human babies are taught how to talk and walk. As a matter of fact, young birds require and receive very little education from their parents. A young bird flies as instinctively as a baby cries.

I saw nothing more of the young hoopoe until the

morning of the 28th April, when I noticed a hoopoe on the roof of my bungalow calling *uk-uk-uk* repeatedly, notwithstanding the fact that it had a caterpillar in its beak. Birds can sing with the mouth full! Presently a young hoopoe appeared on the roof. The adult bird ran to the latter and thrust the caterpillar into its mouth. This was acknowledged by a little squeak of thankfulness.

Most young birds flap their wings and make a great commotion when they think it is time they received a beakful of food. Baby hoopoes, however, do not behave in this way at all. They toddle sedately in the wake of the mother or father, but make no clamour for food. They receive this in a most dignified manner, merely uttering a little squeak of thanks.

To return to the young hoopoe of whose exploits I have been writing. I saw a parent come repeatedly and feed him on the roof of the bungalow on that day and on the 29th and the 30th. This, of course, I was prepared for. But I was not prepared for the next event, which was the revisitation of the nest in the verandah by the two parent birds on the 1st May. On the following days they continued to visit the nest hole, but I had no leisure for watching them. On the 5th May I saw one hoopoe, presumably the cock, literally drive the other into the nest hole. They both flew into the verandah and alighted on a ledge that runs round it a little way below the roof. There the cock emitted some harsh cries, expanded his crest and bowed as described above. Then he advanced towards her. She disappeared into the nest hole. He flew up to the aperture and remained outside on guard for some time. After a little he put his head into the aperture and gave vent to his gentle *uk-uk-uk.* Then he withdrew his head, remained standing outside the nest aperture for a few minutes and flew off. The hen emerged from the hole a couple of minutes later.

The next day the cock was bringing food to the nest, and the hen was apparently incubating. On the 7th, 8th, 9th, 10th, and 11th I saw the cock still at work feeding the hen, uttering at each visit to the nest a soft *coo-coo-coo.* From this date I did not see the cock visit the nest again until the 24th, when I saw him fly to the verandah with some food in his mouth, but he emerged from the nest hole without having disposed of the food he was carrying. He then dropped down on to the lawn and gave this to another hoopoe feeding on the grass. From that day onwards I have not seen a hoopoe visit the nest hole in the verandah. It would seem that after sitting on the second batch of eggs a few days the hen hoopoe went on strike! Or, to speak more correctly, the fury of incubation left her, and she regained her normal taste for a life in the open.

XXXI

THE LARGEST BIRD IN INDIA

IT has always been a cause of wonder and sorrow to me that the sarus crane (*Grus antigone*) does not occur in the neighbourhood of Madras, or indeed in South India at all. The tropical portion of the Indian peninsula, with its millions of acres of green paddy, should be a paradise for cranes; yet not one of these fine birds is likely to be found south of the Godavery, or, at any rate, of the Kistna. There is presumably some good reason for this, but that reason has yet to be discovered.

The sarus might well be called the Indian crane, for it is one of the most characteristic and beautiful birds of Northern India; moreover, it appears to be found nowhere outside India. Saruses occur in Burma, but the Burmese birds have fallen into the hands of the ornithological systematist, and he has, of course, made a separate species of them. The sarus from Burma is now known in the scientific world as *Grus sharpii*—not because very sharp eyes are necessary in order to distinguish him from the Indian form!

The plumage of the sarus is a beautiful shade of

grey. The tail feathers are paler than the rest of the plumage, being almost white in some individuals. There is a broad red band round the neck and the lower part of the head. This at the breeding season becomes very brilliant, and then looks like a broad collar of crimson velvet. The legs of the sarus are also bright red and are nearly a yard long. So that the sarus can, when he wishes to assert himself, look over the head of the average human being without unduly stretching his neck.

The sarus is the only crane that stays in India throughout the year. As has already been said, the species is very common in Northern India; indeed, a broad stretch of landscape in that part of the world would not seem true to life did it not contain a pair of saruses standing near together. Every pair of these birds is a regular Darby and Joan. There are instances on record of a sarus having pined away and died because it had lost its mate. This affection of the male and female who pair for life is so notorious that the Indians who eat the flesh of these birds make a point, after they have bagged one of a pair, of killing the mate.

The food of saruses is, as Hume remarks, very varied. No small reptile or amphibian comes amiss to them. They also eat insects and snails, and seeds and green vegetable matter. They are often to be observed feeding at some distance from water. Indeed, my experience is that they are seen more often on dry land than in water. Their long legs appear to be of little use to them except at the nesting season, when they are necessary in order to enable the birds to wade to the nest. Cranes, unlike storks and herons, cannot grip with the foot, so that they never perch in trees. The nest is built on the ground and, presumably for the sake of protection against jackals, wolves, and such-like creatures, is usually surrounded by water. As a rule, it is not constructed on an island, but is itself an islet rising from the bottom of the *jhil* or tank in which it is situated.

I have not had the good fortune to witness a nest of the sarus in course of construction, but from the behaviour of the owners when heavy rain falls after the nest is completed, I believe that both sexes take part in construction. As the nesting season is in June, July, August, and September, a good deal of rain usually falls while nesting operations are going on. The nest is a mound or cone, composed of rushes and reeds, of which the diameter is two feet at least. The top of this cone, on which the eggs are placed, is usually about a foot above the surface of the water. Thus the eggs lie only a little above the water level; nevertheless, they always feel quite dry, as does the layer of rushes on which they are placed. This is rather surprising—one would expect the water to get soaked up into the parts of the nest above the surface; but this does not happen. It is needless to say that if the top of the nest became submerged it would be impossible to keep the eggs dry; hence, when very heavy rain causes the water level round the nest to rise, the parent saruses raise the top of the nest by adding more material to it.

Two eggs are usually laid. These, as befits the size of the owners, are very large. It is as much as one can do to make both ends meet of a tape eleven inches long, passed round the long axis of the egg. The eggs vary considerably in size, but are usually of a creamy hue, They may be with or without markings. The shell is very thick and hard, so that if sarus's eggs were used for electioneering purposes, fatalities would often occur.

Various observers give very different accounts of the behaviour of the parent saruses when their nest is attacked. The general experience is that they show no fight, but that they retire gracefully as soon as the human being gets within twenty yards of the nest. Hume, however, records one case of a sitting sarus making such vigorous pokes and drives at the man who approached her when sitting on the nest that he was forced to flap her in the face vigorously with his waist cloth before she left her eggs. That, says Hume, is the nearest approach to a fight for its *penates* he has ever seen a sarus make. Recently I visited a nest of these birds, which was situated in a small patch of water, perhaps forty feet square, with a millet field on one side and paddy on the other three. I was on horseback, not wishing to wade nearly to my waist. With me were three men. When we first noticed the nest, the hen was sitting on it and the cock standing near by. As we approached the female rose to her feet very slowly, and then I could see that the nest contained a young one. When we were at a distance of some ten yards the female began to move her feet as if scraping the nest, and the young bird betook itself quietly to the water, and swam slowly into the neighbouring flooded paddy field. The hen then slowly descended from the nest into the water and quietly walked off. On reaching the nest, I found in it one egg. I sent one of the men after the youngster, which he quickly secured and brought to me to look at. It was about the size of a small bazaar fowl, and had perhaps been hatched three days. It was covered with soft down. The down on the upper parts was of a rich reddish fawn colour, the back of the neck, a band along the backbone, and a strip on each wing being the places where the colour was most intense; these were almost chestnut in hue. The lower parts were of a cream colour, into which the reddish fawn merged gradually at the sides of the body. The eyes were large and black. The bill was of pink hue and broad at the base where the yellow lining of the mouth showed. The pink of the bill was most pronounced towards the base, fading almost to white at the tip. The legs and feet were pale pink, the toes being slightly webbed. Even at that stage of the youngster's existence the legs were long, and enabled him to swim with ease, but they were not strong enough to support him when he tried to walk. Sarus cranes cannot walk properly until they are several months old.

While I was handling the young bird the cock sarus was evidently summoning up his courage, for presently he began to advance in battle array, that is to say, with neck bent, so that the head projected forward, mouth slightly open, and wings about half expanded. Thus he slowly approached, looking very handsome. He did not advance direct, but took a circuitous course as if stalking us. When he had approached within about six feet I made a pretence of striking him with a short cane. Of this act of hostility he took not the least notice, but continued to approach. The men with me, who were on foot, began to fear being attacked, so one of them pulled up some paddy stalks and threw these at him. This made him jump and retreat a few paces. But he soon recommenced his advance in battle array. Then one of the men rushed at him. That caused him to retreat a few paces hastily, but with dignity. He then proceeded to attempt a rear attack, and as he circled round us with bent neck he put me in mind of the villain of the melodrama, who stalks about saying "My time will come!" When the sarus had advanced thus to within four feet of my men and looked as though he were about to spring at them, one of these lunged at him with a short stick, and he would have been struck had he not beaten a hasty retreat. Nothing daunted, he again returned to the attack. We were at the nest for fully ten minutes, and the whole time he was trying to get at us. Only once did he utter his trumpet-like call. The female meanwhile remained watching at a distance of perhaps forty yards.

Having seen what we wanted, we replaced the young bird and the egg in the nest and retreated fifteen or twenty yards. We waited to see what the parent birds would do. The female came up to the cock (she is distinguishable by her smaller size); then they both advanced very slowly towards the nest, the hen approaching the faster. When at a distance of perhaps eight yards from the nest, the cock indulged in some curious antics. He slowly drew himself up to his full height and stood thus motionless for a few seconds, then he stretched out his bill towards the sky. Next, the long neck began to bend slowly until it took roughly the shape of the letter S. Then, while the neck was still so bent, the sarus dipped his bill into the water. After this he again stood upright and repeated the whole performance. Finally he indulged in a little dance. Meanwhile the hen slowly advanced, and when within a yard of the nest stood still and contemplated it for a little, then, after caressing the youngster with her bill, she slowly climbed on to the nest. The nest cavity being a very shallow one, the young bird sitting in it could be seen from a considerable distance, and its reddish fawn plumage showed up in strong contrast to its surroundings. The sarus nestling cannot by any stretch of the imagination be called protectively coloured, but it fares very well, notwithstanding its conspicuousness, because its parents never depart far from the nest, and while they are present it is immune from attack. Even large birds of prey avoid the powerful beak of an infuriated crane.

XXXII

THE SWALLOW-PLOVER

TERNS are so beautiful that, where they occur, they are apt to attract unto themselves all attention. This is, I think, the reason why so little is on record regarding the swallow-plovers, which haunt all the larger rivers of India to such an extent that it is scarcely possible to spend an hour on the Ganges, the Jumna, the Gogra, the Indus, the Brahmaputra, the Nerbudda, the Mahanuddy, or even the distant Irawaddy without meeting with a flock of those curious little birds.

Swallow-plovers, or pratincoles, as they are often called, are easily described. They are plovers that subsist largely upon flying insects which they catch when on the wing. As a result of this habit swallow-plovers (*Glareola lactea*) have taken on some of the attributes of the swallow, notably the long wings and the broad gape.

The total length of a swallow-plover, including the tail, is 6½ inches, while the wing alone is nearly six inches long. It is these long wings that give the bird a swallow-like appearance.

The general hue of *Glareola lactea* is that curious

sandy-grey shade of brown which, for some occult reason, is known as isabelline. The short tail is white with a black tip. There is a black streak through the eye and a white one near the margin of the wing. The abdomen is white. The legs are short for those of a plover; nevertheless, the species is very nimble on its feet, and runs in the manner peculiar to the peewit family.

Swallow-plovers are to be found at a distance from water, but they are essentially river birds.

At sunset, when insects in their myriads disport themselves over the surface of rivers, the swallow-plovers issue forth and hawk these flying hexapods just as swallows do, and, as they fly low over the face of the waters, they are doubtless often mistaken for swallows.

Jerdon states that swallow-plovers live exclusively on insects which they catch on the wing. I doubt whether this assertion is correct. These birds certainly feed largely on flying insects, but as they spend the major part of their time on the sand, over which they run swiftly, I think that creeping things constitute a not inconsiderable portion of their diet.

Their nesting habits are similar to those of terns and plovers; that is to say, the eggs are placed on the sand or bare ground without any semblance of a nest.

I make a point every year, if possible, of spending a morning on a river at the beginning of the hot weather looking for the nests of terns and other birds which lay on *churs* and sandbanks. Almost every Indian river is plentifully studded with islets which render its navigation difficult, but afford most convenient nesting sites for many species of birds. The sandy islets whereon eggs are laid are nearly always those of which some portion is sufficiently high to escape being flooded when the river rises in consequence of the melting of the snow on the higher peaks of the Himalayas. The selected islands are almost invariably sufficiently far from the river bank to prevent jackals and other predaceous creatures wading across to them. If terns or plovers fail to take such precautions, the chances are that their eggs will come to grief.

This year (1912), on the 15th April, I went out on the Gogra at Fyzabad, and found over thirty nests of swallow-plovers on one islet, on which I also saw two eggs of the black-bellied tern (*Sterna melanogaster*).

Immediately I set foot on the island the terns and small pratincoles commenced making an uproar, which, of course, amounted to an assurance that they had eggs on the island. One portion of it was well sprinkled with stunted vegetation, and thither I at once repaired, to the great disgust of the swallow-plovers, who flew about excitedly, uttering their lapwing-like cry—*titeri, titeri.* A search of less than a minute served to reveal a couple of eggs placed on the bare ground between two small plants that were growing out of the sand. As I stooped down to examine these eggs I looked round and saw a very curious and pretty sight. Swallow-plovers were surrounding me. They were nearly all on the ground and striking strange attitudes. Some were lying on the sand as though they had been wounded and fallen to the ground; others were floundering on the ground as if in pain; some were fluttering along with one wing stretched out limply, looking as though it were broken; while others appeared to have both wings injured. I did not count the birds, but at least twenty of them were seemingly injured. I had often seen one bird or a pair behave thus, but never a whole flock.

All the plover family have this injury-feigning instinct, but in none is it so well developed as in the pratincoles.

"The strange antics," writes Hume, "played by these little birds, at least those of them that had young or hard-set eggs, whenever we approached their treasures were very remarkable; flying past one, they would come fluttering down on to the sand a few paces in front of one, and there gasp and flutter as if mortally wounded, hobbling on with draggled wings and limping legs as one approached them, and altogether simulating entirely helpless and completely crippled birds. No one unacquainted with the habits of this class of birds could have believed, to see them flapping along on the sands on their stomachs, every now and then falling head over heels and lying quite still for an instant, as if altogether exhausted, that this was all a piece of consummate acting intended to divert our attention from their nests."

Hume here voices the popular opinion that birds, when they behave as though they are injured, are deliberately pretending to be wounded with the object of diverting the attention of an intruder from their eggs or young. I hold this view to be utterly and entirely wrong. Consider the long chain of reasoning that a bird has to make before behaving as swallow-plovers are supposed to do. In the first place the birds must know or believe that the intruder has come with the object of taking their eggs or young ones. They must know or believe that the said intruder would like to capture them in preference to their eggs or young. They must further have discovered that a bird with a leg or a wing broken is easier to capture than one that is sound in limb. They must also know how a bird with a broken wing or leg behaves when endeavouring to escape from a foe. Knowing and believing all these things, the swallow-plover must reason thus within itself: "If I pretend that I am injured the intruder will try to catch me and thus be drawn away from my eggs or young. I will, therefore, proceed to act the wounded bird to the best of my ability."

I do not for a moment believe that the average swallow-plover has half this knowledge and power of reasoning. Its behaviour can be accounted for in a far more probable manner. We all know that instinct teaches birds to fly away from all birds or beasts of prey or large strange moving objects; but instinct teaches them to guard their eggs. Now, when a human being approaches the eggs of a pratincole, these two instincts come into violent opposition, and the bird's mental equilibrium is much disturbed; the result is that the bird undergoes all manner of strange contortions. We look at these and say, "What a clever little bird! How well it is acting!" The contortions of the swallow-plover undoubtedly do tend to attract the attention of predaceous creatures, and are probably useful to the species when there are young, for these are able to slip away while the attention of the attacker is momentarily diverted by the parent birds. Hence such behaviour must tend to be perpetuated by natural selection. That it is in no sense an intelligent act is obvious from the fact that such behaviour occurs when there are eggs, and so can do no good; moreover, the parents will go on behaving in this manner even after the intruder has taken the eggs and put them in his pocket!

Textbooks tell us that *Glareola lactea* lays from two to four eggs. I have never found more than two in a clutch, and think that Hume made a mistake when he said "from two to four," and as plagiarism is very rife among writers on ornithology, other ornithologists have copied his statements without acknowledgment, and, of course, reproduced his mistake!

The eggs of this species are interesting on account of the extraordinary variations they exhibit. As Hume well says, it is scarcely possible to find two eggs (outside the same clutch) that closely resemble each other. It not infrequently happens that the two eggs in the same clutch differ so greatly that it is difficult to believe that they are the produce of one hen. The ground colour may vary from pale green, almost white, to fawn colour. The markings sometimes take the form of blotches, so that the eggs look like those of a small tern. More usually the markings appear as tiny spots, freckles, pencillings, or cloudy smudges. On a sandbank containing twenty nests it is possible to pick out ten eggs, each of which differs so greatly from the others that the casual observer would certainly say they all belonged to different species. The size is, of course, fairly uniform, but the shape varies greatly; some are elongated, while others are nearly as broad as they are long. Occasionally a pear-shaped egg is found, but as a rule the narrow end of the egg is comparatively blunt. That eggs which are laid on the sand in the open should display these extraordinary variations is an awkward fact for those who consider that the colouring of birds' eggs is the direct result of natural selection. If this were so we should expect to find a wonderful sameness about the eggs of this species, which are laid in such exposed situations. The fact is, of course, that on a sandbank eggs of any colour that is not too pronounced are difficult to see; hence, for purposes of protection, the actual colours of the background and the markings of the egg are matters of little importance.

XXXIII

THE BIRDS OF A MADRAS GARDEN

RICHARD JEFFERIES devotes several chapters of one of the most delightful of his books—*Wild Life in a Southern County*—to the birds that frequent a farm on the Downs. "On looking back," he writes, "it appears that the farm-house, garden, orchard, and rickyard at Wick are constantly visited by about thirty-five wild creatures, and, in addition, five others come now and then, making a total of forty. Of these forty, twenty-six are birds, two bats, eight quadrupeds, and four reptiles. This does not include some few additional birds that only come at long intervals, nor those that simply fly overhead or are heard singing at a distance.

"Around the farm-house itself come the starlings, sparrows, swallows, water wagtails, hedge-sparrows, robins, wrens, tomtits, thrushes, and blackbirds. The orchard is frequented by sand martins, cuckoos, missel thrushes, goldfinches, greenfinches, flycatchers, linnets, blackcaps, and titmice.

"In the rickyard are seen redstarts, stone-chats, rooks, chaffinches, wood-pigeons, doves, and larks."

Now a closer observer of nature than Richard Jefferies never existed, and he knew every square yard of the Wick Farm, so that we may be sure that the list he gives is exhaustive.

This list seems very meagre to one who is accustomed to bird life in India. If the Wick Farm were transported bodily and set down in the middle of India it would be visited by seventy or eighty species of birds instead of twenty-six.

Every garden of tolerable size in Madras is the abode of quite twice as many birds as those which visit a downland farm in England, so superior is India to England as a field for the ornithologist.

Every Madrassi whose bungalow is placed in a garden worthy of the name may, without leaving the same, count upon seeing fifty species of birds before he has been many months in the country.

First there are the perennials—the birds which, like the poor, are always with us—the jungle and the house crows, the white-headed babbler, the iora, the red-vented and the white-browed bulbuls, the king-crow, the tailor bird, the common and the brahmany mynas, the common sparrow, the golden-backed woodpecker, the bush lark, Loten's and the purple-rumped sunbirds, the coppersmith, the white-breasted kingfisher, the hoopoe, the koel, the crow-pheasant, the spotted owlet, the common and the brahmany kites, the spotted and the little brown doves, and the cattle egret; while if the garden boast of anything in the shape of a pond there will be found the common kingfisher and the paddy bird.

Nearly all these birds nest in the compound, and all are so familiar to every Anglo-Indian that no description is needed. Moreover, I have, I think, previously treated of all of them with the exception of the iora (*Aegithina tiphia*). In case there be any who are unable to give this beautiful little species a name when they see or hear it, let me briefly describe it. It is considerably smaller than a sparrow, and lives amid the foliage, from which it picks the tiny insects that constitute its food. In summer the upper parts of the cock are black, and the lower parts bright yellow. There are two narrow white bars in the wing. In winter the black on the head and back is replaced by yellowish green. The hen has the upper plumage and tail green, and the lower parts yellow. She also has the two white wing bars. To my mind the iora is a good songster. Nevertheless, "Eha" states that it "has no song, but scarcely any other bird has such a variety of sweet notes." I will not quarrel over the meaning of the word song; every one who knows the iora must agree that it continually makes a joyful noise.

Less common than the birds named above, but occupants of almost every garden, are the butcher birds and their cousins the wood-shrikes, the fantail flycatchers, and the pied wagtails, the emerald bee-eaters, and parakeets, the robin and the palm swift.

The commonest species of butcher bird in Madras is the bay-backed shrike (*Lanius vittatus*), a small bird with a grey head and a maroon back, and a broad black streak through the eye. This tyrant of the garden takes up a perch on a bare branch, and there remains like a sentinel on a watch-tower, until it espies an insect on the ground. On to this it swoops, displaying, as it descends, much white in the wings and the tail.

The wood-shrike (*Tephrodornis pondiceranus*) frequents trees and hedgerows. But for its broad white eyebrow and the white in its tail, it might pass for a sparrow. It is most easily recognised by its melodious and cheerful call—*tanti tuia, tanti tuia.*

The pied wagtail (*Motacilla maderaspatensis*)—elegance personified—loves to sit on the housetop and pour forth a lay which vies with that of the canary. Suddenly away it flies, speeding through the air in undulating flight, until it reaches the ground, where, nimble-footed as Camilla, it chases its insect quarry.

The fantail flycatcher (*Rhipidura albifrontata*) is another study in black and white. This most charming of birds frequents leafy trees, whence it pours forth its sweet song of six or seven notes. Every now and again it, after the manner of all flycatchers, sallies into the air after insects. Having secured its victim, it alights on a branch or on the ground, and there spreads out its tail and turns as if on a pivot, now to one side, now to the other.

We must seek the robin (*Thamnobia fulicata*) among the tangled undergrowth in some corner of the compound neglected by the gardener. There shall we find the pair of them—the cock a glossy black bird with a narrow white bar in the wing, the hen arrayed in a gown of reddish brown. In each sex there is a patch of brick-red feathers under the tail, and, as if for the purpose of displaying this, the tail is carried almost erect.

If there be any fruit ripening, even if it be that of the cypress, green parrots (*Palaeornis torquatus*) are certain to visit the garden. On the approach of a human being these feathered marauders will fling themselves into the air with wild screams, and dash off, looking, as Lockwood Kipling says, like "live emeralds in the sun."

Even more like living emeralds are the little green bee-eaters (*Merops viridis*), whose feeble twitter may emanate from any tree. Take a huge emerald and cut it into the shape of a bird. Insert a pale blue turquoise at the throat, rubies for the eyes, and set these off with strips of darkest emery, let into the head a golden topaz, then breathe into this collection of gems the breath of life, and you will have produced a poor imitation of that gem of the feathered world—the little emerald merops.

If there be palm trees in the garden the presence of the little palm swift (*Tachornis batassiensis*) is assured. Palm swifts are tiny smoky-brown birds which travel unceasingly through the air in pursuit of the insects on which they feed. During flight the wings remain expanded, looking like a bow into the middle of which the slender body is inserted.

I had almost forgotten one of the most striking birds in the world—the Indian paradise flycatcher (*Terpsiphone paradisi*), which certainly is entitled to a place among the common birds of a Madras garden. The cocks are white or chestnut, according to age. The crested head is shining black, and the two median tail feathers are greatly elongated, so that they flutter in the air like satin streamers as the bird flits about among the trees. The hen lacks the lengthened tail feathers, and, as "Eha" says, looks like a chestnut-coloured bulbul. Indeed, Anglo-Indian boys call this species the *Shah Bulbul.*

There are a number of occasional bird visitors to our Madras gardens. Parties of minivets and cuckoo shrikes come and seek for insects among the leaves of trees. The unobtrusive yellow-throated sparrow (*Gymnorhis flavicollis*) is another tree-haunting species to be looked for in the garden. Conspicuous among the less common birds which feed on the ground are the gorgeous roller or "blue jay," the sprightly magpie robin, the white-throated munia, attired like a quaker, and that bird of many colours the Indian pitta, which keeps always near thick underwood, sometimes issuing from thence into the open to give forth a cheery whistle.

In conclusion, mention must be made of the migrant species. Many of the birds that come to the farm on the downs of which Jefferies wrote—the swallows, the cuckoos, and the wagtails—are but summer visitors to England. So do a number of migrating species visit our Madras gardens. There is, however, this difference in the two cases. The migrating species visit England in summer for nesting purposes, whereas they spend the winter in warm Madras, and leave it in summer before the nesting time begins.

Among the winter visitors which come into the garden must be mentioned the beautiful Indian oriole, a study in yellow and black, the Indian redstart, or, to give it its older name, the fire-tail, the grey-headed wagtail, whose under parts are bright yellow, the dull earthy-hued little Sykes's warbler, which hides itself in a bush and keeps on calling out *chick*, and the grey-headed myna, which, but for the fact that the head and recumbent crest are grey, might easily pass for a brahmany myna.

The birds above enumerated do not form by any means an exhaustive list. Were birds that sometimes come into the garden included, the list would extend to three times its present length.

XXXIV

SUNBIRDS

SUNBIRDS, or honey-suckers as they are sometimes called, are to the tropics of the Old World what humming birds are to the warmer portions of the New World.

Sunbirds are tiny feathered exquisites which vary in length from 3½ to 5 inches, including a bill of considerable length for the size of the bird.

They are numbered among the most familiar birds of India, owing to their abundance and their partiality to gardens. They occur all the year round in the warmer parts of the peninsula, but leave the coldest regions for a short time during the winter.

Twenty-nine species of sunbirds are described as belonging to the Indian Empire, but most of them are only local in their distribution. Three species, however, have a considerable range. These are *Arachnechthra asiatica*, the purple sunbird, which occurs throughout India and Burma, ascending the hills to 5000 feet; *A. zeylonica*—the purple-rumped sunbird—which is the commonest sunbird in all parts of Southern India except Madras, where the third species, *A. lotenia*—Loten's sunbird—is perhaps more abundant.

The genus *Arachnechthra* is characterised by a great difference in appearance between the sexes. The hens of all the species are very like one another; all are homely-looking birds, dull greenish brown above and pale yellow below. The cocks of the various species are arrayed in metallic colours as resplendent as those that decorate humming birds.

Seen from a little distance, the cock of the purple-rumped species is a bird with dark head, neck, wings, back, and tail, and bright yellow under parts, while the female is brown above and yellowish beneath. Thus at a distance the male does not look much more beautiful than the female, but if one is able to creep up sufficiently near him his plumage is seen to be unsurpassable; it glistens with a splendid metallic sheen, which is purple or green according to the direction from which the sun's rays fall upon it. On the top of the head is a patch of brilliant shining metallic green, which exceeds in beauty any crown devised by man.

The cocks of the purple and Loten's species are very much alike, but may be readily distinguished by the fact that the slender curved bill of Loten's is considerably longer than that of its cousin. How shall I describe these beautiful birds? In my volume *Indian Birds* I classed them among black birds, because they look black when seen at a distance, but I stated that they are in reality dark purple, and have been taken to task for not classing them among the blue birds. The fact of the matter is that these birds cannot be said to be of any colour; like shot silk, their hue depends upon the angle at which the sun's rays fall upon them. In the sunlight their plumage glistens like a new silk hat, and sometimes the sheen looks lilac and at others green.

The habits of all three species appear to be exactly alike.

The cocks of all have fine voices. At his best the purple sunbird sings as sweetly as a canary. Indeed, on one occasion when I was staying at Bangalore I heard a bird singing in the verandah which I thought was a caged canary; it was only when I went to look at the canary that I discovered it to be a wild sunbird pouring forth its music from some trellis-work!

Sunbirds are always literally bubbling over with energy. They are bundles of vivacity—ever on the move. Although they eat tiny insects, they subsist chiefly on the nectar of flowers, which appears to be a most stimulating diet.

Sunbirds have long, slender, curved bills and tubular tongues, hence they are admirably equipped to secure the honey hidden away in the calyces of flowers. As the little birds insert their heads into the blossoms they get well dusted with pollen, so that, like bees and some other insects, they probably play an important part in the cross-fertilisation of flowers; but they do not hesitate to probe the sides of large flowers with their sharp bills, and thus secure the honey without bearing pollen to the stigma. It is pretty to watch the sunbirds feeding. They are as acrobatic as titmice and strike the most extraordinary attitudes in their attempts to procure honey. When there is no convenient *point d'appui* they hover like humming birds, on rapidly vibrating wings, and while so doing explore with their long tongues the recesses of honeyed flowers. To quote Aitken, "between whiles they skip about, slapping their sides with their tiny wings, spreading their tails like fans, and ringing out their cheery refrain. As they pass from one tree to another they traverse the air in a succession of bounds and sportive spirals." Verily the existence of a sunbird is a happy one!

The nest of the sunbird is one of the most wonderful pieces of architecture in the world, and it is the work of the hen alone. While she is working like a Trojan, her gay young spark of a husband is drinking riotously of nectar! The nest is a hanging one, and is usually suspended from a branch of a bush or a tree, and not infrequently from the rafter of the verandah of an inhabited bungalow; sunbirds show little fear of man.

The nest is commenced by cobwebs being wound round and round the branch from which the nest will hang. Cobweb is the cement most commonly employed by birds. To this pieces of dried grass, slender twigs, fibres, roots, or other material are added and made to adhere by the addition of more cobweb.

The completed nest, which usually hangs in a most conspicuous place, often passes for a small mass of rubbish that has been pitched into a bush, and, in view of the multifarious nature of the material used by the sunbird, there is every excuse for mistaking the nursery for a ball of rubbish. Grasses, fibres, fine roots, tendrils, fragments of bark, moss, lichen, petals or sepals of flowers, in short, anything that looks old and untidy is utilised as building material.

In *Birds of the Plains* I mentioned the sunbirds' nest that was literally covered with the white paper shavings that are used to pack tight the biscuits in Huntley and Palmer's tins.

"It is curious," writes Mr. R. M. Adam, "how fond these birds are of tacking on pieces of paper and here and there a bright-coloured feather from a paroquet or a roller on the outside of their nests. When in Agra a bird of this species built a nest on a loose piece of thatch laid in my verandah, and on the side of the nest, stuck on like a signboard, was a piece of a torn-up letter with 'My dear Adam' on it."

Mr. R. W. Morgan describes a yet more extraordinary nest that was built by sunbirds in an acacia tree in front of his office at Kurnool: "It was ornamented with bits of blotting-paper, twine, and old service stamps that had been left lying about. The whole structure was most compactly bound together with cobwebs, and had a long string of caterpillar excrement wound round it. This excrement had most probably fallen on to a cobweb and had stuck to it, and the cobweb had afterwards been transported in strips to the nest."

The completed nest is a pear-shaped structure, with an opening at one side near the top. Over the entrance hole a little porch projects, which serves to keep out the sun and rain when the nest is exposed to them.

The nest is cosily lined with silk cotton. The aperture at the side acts as a window as well as a door; the hen, who alone incubates, sits on her eggs, looking out of the little window with her chin resting comfortably on the sill.

Two eggs only are laid. The smallness of the clutch indicates that there is not a great deal of loss of life in the nest. The immunity of the sunbird is due chiefly to the inaccessibility of the nest. The latter is usually at the extreme tip of a slender branch upon which no bird of any size can obtain a foothold. When a sunbird does make a mistake and place its nest in an unsuitable place, the predaceous crows devour the young ones, as they did recently in the case of a nest built in the middle of an ingadulsis hedge in my compound at Fyzabad.

In conclusion, I should like to settle one disputed point in the economy of the purple sunbird (*A. asiatica*). Jerdon stated that the cock doffs his gay plumage after the breeding season and assumes a dress like that of the hen except for a purple strip running longitudinally from the chin to the abdomen.

Blanford denied this. He appears to have based his denial on the fact that cocks in full plumage are to be seen at all seasons of the year. There is no month in the year in which I have not seen a cock purple sunbird in nuptial plumage. I used, therefore, to think that Blanford was right and Jerdon wrong.

Afterwards I came across the following passage by

Finn in *The Birds of Calcutta*: "The purple cock apparently thinks his wedding garment too expensive to be worn the whole year round; for after nesting he doffs it, and assumes female plumage, retaining only a purple streak from chin to stomach as a mark of his sex. . . . I well remember one bird which came to the museum compound after breeding to change his plumage; he kept very much to two or three trees, singing, apparently, from one particular twig, and even when in undress he kept up his song."

Since reading the above I have watched purple sunbirds carefully, and have observed that during the months of November and December cocks in full breeding plumage are very rarely seen, although there is no lack of cocks in the eclipse plumage described by Finn.

Moreover, a purple sunbird which is being kept in an aviary in England assumes eclipse plumage for a short period each year at the beginning of winter. Thus there can be no doubt that the cock of the purple species does doff his gay plumage after the nesting season, but only for a short period. In January the majority of cocks are in breeding plumage, and, indeed, in some parts of the country nest building begins as early as February.

XXXV

THE BANK MYNA

THE bank myna (*Acridotheres ginginianus*), like the Indian corby (*Corvus macrorhynchus*), is a bird that has suffered neglect at the hands of those who write about the feathered folk. The reason of this neglect is obvious. Even as the house crow (*Corvus splendens*) overshadows the corby, so does the common myna (*Acridotheres tristis*) almost eclipse the bank myna. So familiar is the myna that all books on Indian birds deal very fully with him. They discourse at length upon his character and his habits, and then proceed to dismiss the bank myna with the remark that his habits are those of his cousin.

The bank myna is a myna every inch of him. He is a chip of the old block; there is no mistaking him for anything but what he is. So like to his cousin is he that when I first set eyes upon him I took him for a common myna freak. And I still believe I was not greatly mistaken. I submit that the species arose as a mutation from *A. tristis*.

Once upon a time a pair of common mynas must have had cause to shake their heads gravely over one or more of their youngsters who differed much from the rest of the brood. As these youngsters grew up, the differences became even more marked, they showed themselves slaty grey where they should have been rich brown, and pinkish buff where white feathers ought to have appeared, and the climax must have been reached when these weird youngsters developed crimson patches of skin at the sides of the head, instead of yellow ones. Probably, the other mynas of the locality openly expressed their disapproval of these caricatures of their species, for mynas do not keep their feelings to themselves. As likely as not they put these new-fangled creatures into Coventry, for birds are as conservative as old maids.

Thus these myna freaks were compelled to live apart, but, being strong and healthy, they throve and either paired *inter se*, or managed to secure mates among their normally dressed fellows. In either case, the offspring bore the stamp of their abnormal parents.

It is a curious fact, and one which throws much light on the process of evolution, that abnormalities have a very strong tendency to perpetuate themselves. Thus was brought into being a new species, and as there were in those times no ornithologists to shoot these freaks, and as they passed with credit the test prescribed by nature, the species has secured a firm footing in India. This hypothesis accounts for the comparatively restricted distribution of the bank myna. It does not occur south of the Narbada and Mahanadi Rivers, but is found all over the plains of Northern India, and ascends some way up the Himalayas. It is particularly abundant in the eastern portion of the United Provinces. In the course of a stroll through the fields at Allahabad, Lucknow, or Fyzabad, one meets with thousands of bank mynas. There seems to be evidence that this species is extending its range both eastwards and westwards; and one of these days a southerly advance may be made, so that eventually the bank myna may form an attractive addition to the birds of Madras.

This species goes about in flocks of varying numbers, after the fashion of the common myna. It comes into towns and villages, but is much less of a garden bird than its familiar cousin. It is in the fields, especially in the vicinity of rivers, that these birds occur most abundantly. They consort with all the other species of myna, for, whatever may have been thought of them when first evolved, they are now in society. King-crows (*Dicrurus ater*) dance attendance upon them as they do on the common mynas, for the sake of the insects put up by them as they strut through the grass. The king-crow, owing to the length of its tail and the shortness of its legs, is no pedestrian, and so is not able to beat for itself.

The books tell us that bank mynas feed on insects, grain, and fruit. I am inclined to think that their diet is confined almost exclusively to the first of these articles. I speak not as one having authority, for, in order to do this, it is necessary to shoot dozens of the birds and carefully examine the contents of their stomachs. This kind of thing I leave to the economic ornithologist. I admit that bank mynas are very partial to the fields of millet and other tall grain crops, but I am persuaded that they visit these for the insects that lurk on their spikes.

Grasshoppers are to the common myna what bread and meat are to the Englishman, the *pièces de résistance* of the menu. This is why mynas always affect pasture land, where it exists, and keep company with cattle, the sedate march of which causes so much consternation among the grasshoppers. Bank mynas eat grasshoppers, but seem to prefer other insects, especially those which lurk underground.[1] Certain it is that wherever they occur they maintain a sharp look-out for the ploughman, and follow him most assiduously as he turns up the soil by means of his oxen-drawn plough. The house crows also attend this function. The other species of myna follow the plough, but not so consistently as the bank myna. The pied starling, although it does not disdain the insects cast up by the plough, seems to prefer to pick its food out of mud. One often sees a flock of these birds paddling about in shallow water, as though they were sandpipers.

It is amusing to watch a flock of bank mynas strutting along a newly turned furrow. In Upper India it is usual for two or more ploughs to work

[1] Since the above was written, C. W. Mason has published a paper entitled *The Food of Birds in India.* In this he shows that eight stomachs of the bank myna contained 106 insects. His researches show that this species is very partial to the caterpillars of the common castor pest, *Ophiusa melicerte. Vide Memoirs of the Department of Agriculture in India* (Entomological Series, Vol. III).

together in Indian file, a few yards separating them. The mynas like to place themselves between two ploughs, and so fearless are they that they sometimes allow themselves almost to be trodden on by the team behind them. Although the progress of the ploughing oxen is not rapid, it is too fast for the mynas, who find themselves continually dropping behind, and have every now and again to use their wings to keep pace with them. At intervals, the whole following, or a portion of it, takes to its wings and indulges in a little flight purely for the fun of the thing. The flock sometimes returns to the original plough, at others transfers its attentions to another. Thus the flocks are continually changing in number and personnel, and in this respect are very different from the companies of seven sisters. The latter appear to be definite clubs or societies, the former mere chance collections of individuals, or probably pairs of individuals.

Bank mynas are so called because they invariably nest in sandbanks, in the sides of a well, or some such locality, they themselves excavating the nest hole. Like sand martins, bank mynas breed in considerable companies, but they are not so obliging as regards the season of their nidification. They usually select sites which are not only at a distance from human habitations, but difficult of access, and, as the birds do not begin to nest until well on in May, when the weather in Upper India is too hot to be described in literary language, one does not often have a chance of seeing the birds at work. Their nesting passages do not necessarily run inwards in a straight line. The result is that neighbouring ones often communicate. At the end of the passage is a circular chamber which is lined with grass and anything else portable. Cast-off snake skin is a lining particularly sought after. Mr. Jesse informs us that from one of these nests in the bank of the Goomti, near Lucknow, he extracted parts of a Latin exercise and some arithmetic questions. The owners of the nest were not going in for higher education; it was merely a case of putting a thing to a use for which it was never intended, a feat at which both birds and Indian servants are great adepts. Notwithstanding the fact that the eggs are laid in dark places, they are blue, as are those of the other mynas. Young bank mynas lack the red skin at the side of the head, and are brown in places where the adults are black. Young mynas of all species have a rather mangy appearance. Like port wine, they improve with age.

XXXVI

THE JACKDAW

THE jackdaw, although numbered among the birds of India, has not succeeded in establishing itself in the plains. Large numbers of jackdaws visit the Punjab in winter, where they keep company with the house crows and the rooks, the three species appearing to be on the best of terms. At the first approach of the warm weather the daws, the rooks, and the majority of the ravens betake themselves to Kashmir or to Central Asia, leaving the house crows to represent the genus *Corvus* in the plains of the Punjab. The jackdaw (*Corvus monedula*) is in shape and colouring like our friend *Corvus splendens*, differing only in its smaller size and in having a white iris to the eye. As is the case with the common Indian crow, individual jackdaws differ considerably in the intensity of the greyness of the neck. In some specimens the sides of the neck are nearly white. Of these systematists have made a new species, which they call *C. collaris*. Oates, I am glad to observe, declines to recognise this species. A jackdaw is a jackdaw all the world over, and it is absurd to try to make him anything else.

As it has not been my good fortune to spend any time in Kashmir, my acquaintance with the jackdaws of India is confined to those that visit the Punjab in winter. These do not appear to frequent the vicinity of houses; I have invariably found them feeding in fields at some distance from a village. They roost, along with the crows and the rooks, in remote parts of the country. Every evening during the half-hour before sunset two great streams of birds pass over Lahore. The larger stream, consisting of crows, rooks, and daws, moves in a north-westerly direction, while the other, composed exclusively of ravens, takes a more westerly course. The ravens apparently decline to consort with their smaller and more frivolous relations.

Although jackdaws seem never to remain in the plains after the beginning of spring, they are able to thrive well enough in the hot weather. A specimen in the Zoological Gardens at Lahore keeps perfectly well, and loses none of his high spirits even when the heat is, to use the words of Kipling, "enough to make your bloomin' eyebrows crawl." But then, as Bishop Stanley asked, "who ever saw or heard of a moping, melancholy jackdaw?" This particular bird is able to hold his own quite well against the crows, rooks, and ravens confined in the same aviary. Moreover, all these are on quite friendly terms with an Australian piping crow—a butcher bird which apes the manners and appearance of a crow so successfully as to delude the *Corvi* into thinking that he is one of themselves! Half a century ago Jerdon wrote: "The jackdaw is tolerably abundant in Kashmir and in the Punjab, in the latter country in the cold weather only. It builds in Kashmir in old ruined palaces, holes in rocks, beneath roofs of houses, and also in trees, laying four to six eggs, dotted and spotted with brownish black." No one living in Kashmir appears to have taken the trouble to amplify this somewhat meagre account of the jackdaw in Asia. It would be interesting to know whether the daws of Kashmir have any habits peculiar to themselves. The fact that Jerdon mentions their breeding in trees is interesting, for in England they nest in buildings in nine hundred and ninety-nine cases out of a thousand.

The jackdaw makes a most admirable pet. When taken young it becomes remarkably tame, soon learning to follow its master about like a dog. Moreover, the bird is as full of tricks as is a wagon-load of monkeys, so that Mr. Westell does not exaggerate when he says that the jackdaw when kept as a pet seems more of an imp than a bird. It thieves for the mere sake of thieving. The nest is sometimes a veritable museum of curiosities. One bird, immortalised by Bishop Stanley, appears to have tried to convert its nest into a draper's shop, for this, although not finished, was found to contain some lace, part of a worsted stocking, a silk handkerchief, a frill, a child's cap, " besides several other things, but so ragged and worn out that it was impossible to make out what they were."

XXXVII

FIGHTING IN NATURE

A CORRESPONDENT to *Country Life* states that he has noticed that in the various battles between ravens and golden eagles, which frequently take place in the island of Skye, the golden eagles are always defeated.

He enquires whether this phenomenon is a usual one and how it is that the comparatively weak raven can vanquish so powerful a bird as the golden eagle.

The above statement and its attendant queries are the result of faulty observation.

Such a thing as a battle between ravens and golden eagles has probably never happened. If it did take place it could have but one ending—the victory of the golden eagles.

Battles rarely, if ever, occur in nature between different species. In order that a battle may take place it is necessary that each of the opposing species should want the same thing and be ready to fight and, if necessary, to sustain serious injuries in order to obtain that thing.

Now these conditions are rarely fulfilled except at the breeding season, when males of the same species fight for the females.

The only other things over which fighting is likely to arise are food and nesting sites.

It frequently happens that birds of different species want the same food. But this rarely leads to anything in the nature of a battle. In such contests the weaker almost invariably gives way to the stronger without any fighting.

A familiar instance of this is afforded by the behaviour of the white-backed (*Pseudogyps bengalensis*) and the black vultures (*Otogyps calvus*) when they gather round a carcase.

Jesse writes, and my experience bears out what he says: "Often I have been watching the vulgar white-backed herd, with a disreputable following of kites and crows, teasing and fighting over a body, when one of these aristocrats (i.e. *Otogyps calvus*), in his red cap and white waistcoat, has made his appearance. Way is immediately made for him, the plebeian herd slinking back as if ashamed or afraid, and I cannot remember the last comer ever being obliged to assert his authority."

If the smaller vultures, which are the more numerous, chose to combine, they could drive off the black vultures, but in doing this some of them would run the risk of sustaining injuries. Now, it seems to be a rule in nature that no creature will willingly run such a risk. Rather than do this an animal will flee before a comparatively puny adversary.

The instinct of self-preservation, which includes the preservation of the body from injury, is strongly developed in all organisms. Natural selection tends to develop this instinct, because the individuals in which the instinct is strongly developed are less likely to be injured by fighting than those which are pugnacious. In other words, it does not pay to fight in nature. Injured individuals are seriously handicapped in the struggle for existence. Thus natural selection tends to produce cowards.

At the breeding season an instinct, which is ordinarily dormant in birds, suddenly becomes active—the instinct of preserving the nest and its contents.

This instinct, when aroused, frequently overmasters the instinct of self-preservation, with the result that shy birds become bold, timid ones grow aggressive, little birds which usually are terrified at the close proximity of a human being allow themselves to be handled rather than leave their eggs or young.

At the breeding season the desire to protect the nest leads many birds to attack, or to make as if to attack, all intruders.

No sight is commoner in India than that of a pair of little drongos (*Dicrurus ater*) chasing a kite or a crow.

Similarly I have witnessed doves chase and put to flight a tree-pie (*Dendrocitta rufa*), and fantail flycatchers mob a corby (*Corvus macrorhynchus*).

Nor are such cases confined to India.

In England Mr. A. H. Bryden states that he has seen sea-gulls mob and put to flight so formidable a creature as a peregrine falcon.

In each of the above instances the bird pursued could, if it wished, turn round and rend its puny adversaries. Why does it not do so? Because the instinct of self-preservation is implanted in it so firmly.

This instinct teaches it never to resist an attack, no matter how feeble the attacker be.

The object of the attack, provided it have no nest to defend, has everything to lose and nothing to gain by resisting the attack and giving battle. It matters little to a golden eagle on the look-out for quarry in which direction it flies; hence if, while it is sailing through the air, it is suddenly attacked by a couple of infuriated ravens, the obvious course is for it to change the direction of its flight. If it fail to do this it must either run the risk of being severely pecked by the ravens or fight them and thereby expose itself to injury. Under the circumstances it naturally chooses the line of least resistance.

It is absurd to speak of a bird that behaves in this manner as being defeated in battle. It does not suffer defeat. It merely declines to give battle.

The general rule in nature is, "Never fight when a fight can be avoided."

This rule is unconsciously followed by all birds, except those that have nests.

The most familiar example of the rule in operation is the well-known habit of birds of surrendering their perches to new-comers. When individual A flies to a perch occupied by individual B the latter almost invariably gives way without demur. The particular perch is of no value to the occupier, but a whole body may be a matter of life or death.

XXXVIII

BIRDS AND BUTTERFLIES

BIOLOGICAL science is at present in a rather peculiar position. Biologists are divided into two parties. On the one side stand the theorists and their followers; on the other the practical men who think for themselves. At present, the theorists are the party in power (and they are quite Lloyd-Georgian in their methods), while the practical men, the breeders and the field naturalists, form the opposition. The reason of the division is that many facts, that have come to light lately, do not fit in with the theories that hold the field.

Now, when facts are discovered which militate against a theory the proper course for the holder of the theory is to test carefully the alleged facts, and if they prove to be really facts to discard or modify his theory. Unfortunately the professional biologists of to-day do not usually follow this course. They have made fetishes of their theories, which they worship as the Israelites worshipped the golden calf. The consequence is that they feel in honour bound either to ignore or to gloss over the facts that are subversive of their fetishes. When they write books in honour of their fetishes, they omit many facts which tend to show that their fetishes are shams. They regard the discussers of the awkward facts as enemies to be crushed. Hence the gulf between the two classes of biologists.

One of the fetishes of the present day is the theory of protective mimicry. Butterflies and moths are the organisms which exemplify best this theory.

It often happens that two species of butterfly occur in the same locality which resemble one another in outward appearance. In such cases zoologists assert that one species mimics the other. They maintain that this mimicry has been brought about by natural selection, because the one species profits by aping its neighbour. The species that is copied is said to be unpalatable. The copy-cat, if I may use the expression, may be either palatable or unpalatable. In either case it is believed to profit by the resemblance. If it is edible the birds that are supposed to prey upon butterflies are said to leave it alone, because they mistake it for its unpalatable neighbour. This resemblance of an edible form to an unpalatable one is called Batesian mimicry.

If the copy-cat be unpalatable it is nevertheless said to profit by the likeness, because young birds are supposed to feed on every kind of butterfly and only to learn by experience which are unpalatable. The theory is that if they attack a red-coloured butterfly and find it nasty to the taste, they leave all red-coloured butterflies alone henceforth. Thus, the imitating species may benefit by the sacrifice of the other red-coloured species. This is known as Mullerian mimicry.

The mimicry theory is very enticing; indeed, it is so enticing that those who hold it, as, for example, Professor Poulton, of Oxford, seem to think that there *must* be something wrong with the evidence opposed to it.

I assert that it is not the evidence against the theory, but the theory itself that is wrong.

The objections to the hypothesis are many and weighty. Finn and I summarised most of them in *The Making of Species.*

Two of the objections appear to be insuperable.

The likeness cannot be of much use until it is fairly strong. How, then, is the beginning of the resemblance to be explained?

In order that natural selection should have produced these astounding resemblances, it is necessary that butterflies should be preyed on very largely by birds; but all the evidence goes to show that birds very rarely eat butterflies. In the course of some ten years spent in India I have not seen butterflies chased by birds on more than a dozen occasions. Similarly, Colonel Yerbury, during six years' observation in India and Ceylon, can record only about six cases of birds capturing, or attempting to capture, butterflies. Colonel C. T. Bingham, in Burma, states that between 1878 and 1891 he on two occasions witnessed the systematic hawking of butterflies by birds, although he observed on other occasions some isolated cases.

Nor is the evidence, as regards India, confined to the experience of the casual observer. Mr. C. W. Mason, when supernumerary entomologist to the

Imperial Department of Agriculture for India, conducted a careful enquiry into the food of birds. The enquiry was made at Pusa in Bengal, in the years 1907, 1908, 1909. The results arrived at by Mr. Mason are published in the *Memoirs of the Department of Agriculture for India* (Entomological Series, Vol. III, January, 1912). As the result of this enquiry, in the course of which the contents of the stomachs of hundreds of Indian birds were examined, Mr. Mason writes (page 338, *loc. cit.*) : "Butterflies do not form any appreciable proportion of the food of any one species of bird, though a good many birds take these insects at times. . . .

"The butterflies include a number of minor pests, of which *Melanitis ismene* was taken by *Merops viridis* and *Papilio pammon* by *Acridotheres tristis.* Other well-known pests are *Pieris brassicae, Virachola isocrates* and *Papilio demoleus. Belenois mesentina,* a Pierid, was seen to be taken on one occasion by the king-crow, and *Ilerda sena* by *Passer domesticus,* both of which insects are neutral.

"Moths include many major pests of varied habits —defoliators, miners, cut-worms, grain and fabric pests. The larvae form an inexhaustible supply of insect food to almost all species of insectivorous birds, and even many species of birds that when mature feed almost, if not quite, entirely on grain and seeds are when in the nest fed very largely on caterpillars by the parent birds."

Obviously, then, in India birds comparatively rarely attack butterflies; but they devour millions of caterpillars. It is the same in other parts of the world.

Mr. G. A. K. Marshall, in the course of five years' observation in South Africa, recorded eight cases of birds capturing butterflies.

Similarly Mr. Banta points out in various issues of *Nature*, in 1912, that all the evidence available shows that in North America birds very rarely capture butterflies. Field naturalists scarcely ever witness a butterfly chased by a bird. Of 40,000 stomachs of birds examined very few were found to contain remains of butterflies.

In 1911 the butterflies of the species *Eugonia californica* were so numerous that " the ground was often blackened with them, and great swarms of them filled the air from morning to evening." Yet of the birds in the locality where those butterflies were most numerous, only five out of forty-five species were found by direct observation and stomach examination to eat the eugonia, and the only bird that fed off them copiously was the brewer blackbird (*Euphagus cyanocephalus*) which is almost omnivorous, and eats insects of all kinds, even if they be what Darwinians call warningly coloured!

Now, modern theorists, as a rule, ignore facts such as these, and this certainly is the wisest course they can pursue, unless they are ready to give up these theories or make themselves look foolish.

However, I am glad to be able to record that Professor Poulton has, as regards the remarks of Mr. Banta, not followed the usual course of the modern theorist.

He has had the courage to take up the cudgels and reply to Mr. Banta in *Nature*. The reason of this unusual course appears to be that Mr. C. F. M. Swynnerton has made some observations in South Africa which Professor Poulton considers are in favour of his pet theory.

According to the Professor, Mr. Swynnerton, as the result of three and a half years' investigation in South-East Rhodesia, "has obtained the records of nearly 800 attacks made by 35 species of birds belonging to 30 genera and 18 families, upon 79 species of butterflies belonging to 9 families or sub-families."

Professor Poulton does not seem to see that the researches of Mr. Swynnerton are altogether subversive of the theory of protective mimicry. In order that natural selection may totally change the colouring of a butterfly (as it does according to the theory of protective mimicry), that butterfly must be habitually preyed upon by large numbers of birds, which must be so vigilantly and unceasingly on the look-out for it, that its only chance of escaping from their attacks must be for it to assume a disguise.

Compare with this the state of affairs revealed by Mr. Swynnerton's observations. He worked for three and a half years, and, as his investigations extended to eighteen families of birds, they must have been very extensive. Exactly how extensive they have been we do not know, because he has not yet published them. Nevertheless, as the result of three and a half years' watching and stomach examination he has evidence of only "nearly 800" attacks made by birds on insects; that is to say, on an average about two attacks in three days!

Watch a bee-eater feeding and you will see it take twenty or thirty insects in less than an hour. If you were to watch it one whole day you might see it capture 300 insects, but certainly not more than one of its victims, on an average, would be a butterfly. Yet, the theory of mimicry is based upon the assumption that butterflies are so greatly preyed upon by birds that they require special means of protection!

I ask all who are interested in the subject to be ever on the look-out for birds chasing butterflies or moths. These are so large and so easy to identify that there can be no chance of mistaking them. Even a casual observer, when watching a bird, cannot fail to notice the capture of a butterfly by it. And when a bird has captured a butterfly it cannot dispose of it very quickly. According to Mr. Swynnerton, "some (birds) swallow the insect (butterfly or moth) whole, but usually after masticating or beating it; some remove inconvenient portions by 'worrying' like a dog or beating against perch or ground; some grasp the prey in one foot and tear off the rejected portions with the bill, eating the rest piecemeal."

The fact that the average bird has to go through all the above performances before devouring a creature containing so little nourishment as a butterfly, is sufficient to show that it does not pay birds to chase butterflies.

But it is best not to rely on arguments to refute the theories of persons who have no logic in them.

The only way to destroy the pernicious zoological theories that hold the field at present is to pile up the facts that tell against them. Similarly, theories that are true cannot be established satisfactorily except by the accumulation of facts. The relations between birds and butterflies can be determined only by observation, and for that kind of observation no country presents a better field than India. Moreover, such observations can be conducted by people having little or no scientific knowledge.

XXXIX

VOICES OF THE NIGHT

THE stillness of the Indian night suffers many interruptions.

In the vicinity of a town or village the hours of darkness are rendered hideous by the noises of human beings and of their appendages—the pariah dogs. In the jungle the " friendly silences of the moon " are continually disturbed by the bark of the fox, the yelling of the jackal, or the notes of the numerous birds of the night.

The call of the various nocturnal birds must be familiar to every person who has spent a hot weather in the plains of Northern India and slept night after night beneath the starry heavens. With the calls of the birds all are familiar, but some do not know the names of the originators of these sounds.

First and foremost of the fowls that lift up their voices after the shades of night have fallen are the tiny spotted owlets (*Athene brama*). Long before the sun has set these quaint little creatures emerge from the holes in which they have spent the day, and treat the neighbours to a " torrent of squeak and chatter and gibberish " which is like nothing else in the world, and which Tickell has attempted to syllabise as "*Kucha, kwachee, kwachee, kwachee, kwachee*," uttered as rapidly as the little owlets' breath will allow of. These noisy punchinellos are most vociferous during moonlit nights, but they are by no means silent in the dark portion of the month.

Almost as abundant as the spotted owlet is another feathered pigmy—the jungle owlet (*Glaucidium radiatum*). This species, like the last, calls with splendid vigour. Fortunately for the Anglo-Indian its note is comparatively mellow and musical. It is not altogether unlike the noise made by a motor cycle when it is being started, consisting, as it does, of a series of disyllables, low at first with a pause after each, but gradually growing in intensity and succeeding one another more rapidly until the bird seems to have fairly got away, when it pulls up with dramatic abruptness. The best attempt to reduce to writing the call of this bird is that of Tickell: "*Turtuck, turtuck, turtuck, turtuck, turtuck, turtuck, tukatu, chatuckatuckatuck.*" This owlet calls in the early part of the night and at intervals throughout the period of darkness, and becomes most vociferous just before the approach of "rosy-fingered dawn."

Very different is the cry of the little scops owl (*Scops giu*). This bird has none of that Gladstonian flow of eloquence which characterises the spotted and the jungle owlets. His note is, however, more befitting the dignity of an owl. He speaks only in monosyllables, and gives vent to those with great deliberation. He sits on a bough and says "*wow*" in a soft but decisive manner. When this pronouncement has had time to sink into the ears of his listeners, he repeats "*wow,*" and continues to sound this impressive monotone at intervals of a minute for several hours.

The above are the three owls which are most often heard in the plains of Northern India. Sometimes all three species, like the orators in Hyde Park, address the world simultaneously from neighbouring trees.

There are numbers of other owls that disturb the stillness of the night with more or less vigour, but it would be tedious, if not impossible, to describe them all. It must suffice to make mention of the low, solemn booming *durgoon durgoon*, of the huge rock-horned owl (*Bubo bengalensis*) and the wheezy screech of the barn owl (*Strix flammea*).

Another call, often heard shortly before dawn, is doubtless usually believed to be that of an owl. This is the deep, *whoot, whoot, whoot* of the coucal or crow pheasant (*Centropus sinensis*), that curious chocolate-winged black ground-cuckoo which builds its nest in a dense thicket.

Unfortunately for the peace of mankind the coucal is not the only cuckoo that lifts up its voice in the night. Three species of cuckoo exist in India which are nocturnal as owls, as diurnal as crows, and as noisy as a German band. A couple of hours' sleep in the hottest part of the day appears to be ample for the needs of these super-birds. From this short slumber they awake, like giants refreshed, to spend the greater portion of the remaining two-and-twenty hours in shrieking at the top of their voices.

Needless to state these three species are the brain-fever bird, the koel, and the Indian cuckoo—a triumvirate that it is impossible to match anywhere else in the world. Some there are who fail to distinguish between these three giants, and who believe that they are but one bird with an infinite variety of notes. This is not so. They are not one bird, but three birds. Let us take them in order of merit.

The brain-fever bird or hawk cuckoo (*Hierococcyx varius*) is *facile princeps.* In appearance it is very like a sparrow-hawk, and, but for its voice, it might be mistaken for one. This species has two distinct notes. The first of these is well described by Cunningham as a "highly pitched, trisyllabic cry, repeated many times in ascending semitones until one begins to think, as one sometimes does when a Buddhist is repeating his ordinary formula of prayer, that the performer must surely burst." But the brain-fever bird never does burst. He seems to know to a scruple how much he may with safety take out of himself. It is not necessary to dilate upon this note. Have we not all listened to the continued screams of "brain-fever, *brain-fever*, BRAIN-FEVER," until we began to fear for our reason? The other call is in no way inferior in magnitude. It consists of a volley of single descending notes, uttered with consummate ease—*facilis descensus*—which may or may not, at the option of the performer, be followed by one or more mighty shouts of BRAIN-FEVER. There is not an hour in the twenty-four during the hot weather when this fiend does not make himself heard in the parts of the country haunted by him. His range extends from Naini Tal to Tuticorin and from Calcutta to Delhi. Assam, Sind, and the Punjab appear to be the only portions of India free from this cuckoo.

The second of the great triumvirate is the Indian koel (*Eudynamis honorata*). This noble fowl has three calls, each as powerful as the others.

The first is a crescendo *ku-il, ku-il, ku-il,* very pleasing to Indian ears, but too powerful for the taste of Westerns. The second is well described by Cunningham as an outrageous torrent of shouts, sounding "*kuk, kŭū, kŭū, kŭū, kŭū, kŭū,*" repeated at brief intervals in tones loud enough to wake the seven sleepers. When the bird thus calls its whole body vibrates with the effort put forth. The third cry is uttered only when the koel is being chased by angry crows, and is, as Cunningham says, a mere cataract of shrill shrieks: "*Hekaree, karee.*"

For the benefit of those unacquainted with the ways of the koel it is necessary to state that that bird spends much of its time fleeing before the wrath of crows. It lays its eggs in the nests of these. And, if one may judge from their behaviour, they suspect the koel. The other two calls are heard at all hours of the day and night, and it makes no difference to the koel whether it is the sun or the moon, or only the stars that are shining. He is always merry and bright. The second call, however, is usually reserved for the dawn. Hence this particular vocal effort is rendered all the more exasperating, coming as it does precisely at the time when, after the departure of a "sable-vested night" straight from Dante's Inferno, which has been embellished by the sluggishness of the *punkawalla*, a certain degree of coolness sets in to give some chance of a little refreshing sleep. Then is it that the jaded dweller in the plains, uttering strange oaths, rushes for his gun and seeks out the disturber of his slumber. In case there be any unable to identify the koel, let it be said that the cock is black from head to foot, that he possesses a wicked-looking red eye, that he is about the size of a crow, but has a slighter body and a longer tail. The hen is speckled black and white. This bird spares not even Sind or the Punjab. It visits every part of the plains of India, wintering in the south and summering in the north.

The third of the triumvirate, the common Indian cuckoo (*Cuculus micropterus*), although in its way a very fine bird, is not of the same calibre as its *confrères*. It stands to them in much the same relation as Trinity College, Dublin, does to the Universities of Oxford and Cambridge. It has quite a pleasant note, which Indians represent as *Boutotaku*, but which is perhaps better rendered by the words "wherefore, therefore," repeated with musical cadence. It does not call much during the middle of the day. It usually uplifts its voice about two hours before sunset, and continues until the sun has been up for a couple of hours. This cuckoo is very common in the Himalayas and in the plains of India from Fyzabad to Calcutta. Fyzabad ought really to be renamed Cuckooabad. It is the habitation of untold numbers of cuckoos. There during the merry month of May the cuckoos spend the night chanting anthems of which the refrain runs *kui-il, ku-il, ku-il, wherefore, therefore, brain-fever, brain-fever, brain-fever.* The Indian cuckoo is very like the English cuckoo in appearance, and it victimises the seven sisters (*Crateropus canorus*) and other babblers, as does the brain-fever bird.

The night-loving cuckoos have demanded so much space that the other vocalists of the hours of darkness will have to be content with very brief notice.

The night heron (*Nycticoran griseus*) makes the welkin ring with his guttural cries of "*waak, waak,*" uttered as he flies after nightfall from his roost to the pond where he will fish till morning. As he fishes in silence the addition he makes to the noises of the night is not great. The large family of plovers must be dismissed in a single sentence. They, like many cuckoos, regard sleep as a luxury; hence their plaintive cries are heard both by day and by night. The most familiar of their calls is the "*did-he-do-it, pity-to-do-it,*" of the red-wattled lapwing (*Sarcogrammus indicus*). The notes the rest of his family consist of variations of the words *titeri, titeri.*

In conclusion, mention must be made of the nightjars or goatsuckers, as they are sometimes called after the fashion of the Romans, who believed that these birds used to sally forth at night and milk goats. This belief was based on two facts. First, the udders of goats were often found to be empty in the morning; secondly, the broad gape possessed by the nightjar. However, the character of these birds has now been cleared. We know that their bills are wide in order to seize large insects on the wing, and that if goats yield no milk in the morning it is not the nightjar who is to blame. Nightjars are brownish grey birds, mottled and barred all over like cuckoos, for which they are often mistaken. Two are common in India. The first of these is *Caprimulgus asiaticus*, the common Indian nightjar, whose call is heard only after nightfall, and resembles the sound made by a stone skimming over ice. The other nightjar is that of Horsfield (*Caprimulgus macrurus*). Its note has been compared to the noise made by striking a plank with a hammer. The distribution of nightjars is capricious. They are fairly common in the western districts of the United Provinces.

Horsfield's nightjar is abundant in the *sal* forests of the Pilibhit district.

INDEX

INDEX